BOUNDARIES, POWER AND ETHICAL RESPONSIBILITY

IN COUNSELLING AND PSYCHOTHERAPY

ESSENTIAL ISSUES IN COUNSELLING AND PSYCHOTHERAPY

Edited by Andrew Reeves

Counsellors and psychotherapists consider a number of important factors in their work with clients. Some are defined by training and theoretical orientation, some by context, and others by the client group with whom they work. However, across all these areas there are a number of essential issues – those that sit at the very core of practice – that must be considered by all therapists.

Essential Issues in Counselling and Psychotherapy is a series that brings together a number of new, accessible and practice-informed books that carefully and thoroughly address those considerations: the essential issues of practice that can challenge and shape all aspects of counselling and psychotherapy.

For new and forthcoming books in the series please visit www.uk.sagepub.com/cp

Assessment and Case Formulation in Counselling and Psychotherapy
Biljana van Rijn

The Therapeutic Relationship in Counselling and Psychotherapy
Rosanne Knox and Mick Cooper

Working with Risk in Counselling and Psychotherapy
Andrew Reeves

BOUNDARIES, POWER AND ETHICAL RESPONSIBILITY

IN COUNSELLING AND PSYCHOTHERAPY

BY

KIRSTEN AMIS

⑤SAGE

Los Angeles | London | New Delhi
Singapore | Washington DC | Melbourne

⑤SAGE

Los Angeles | London | New Delhi
Singapore | Washington DC | Melbourne

SAGE Publications Ltd
1 Oliver's Yard
55 City Road
London EC1Y 1SP

SAGE Publications Inc.
2455 Teller Road
Thousand Oaks, California 91320

SAGE Publications India Pvt Ltd
B 1/I 1 Mohan Cooperative Industrial Area
Mathura Road
New Delhi 110 044

SAGE Publications Asia-Pacific Pte Ltd
3 Church Street
#10-04 Samsung Hub
Singapore 049483

Library of Congress Control Number: 2016954635

British Library Cataloguing in Publication data

A catalogue record for this book is available from the
British Library

Editor: Susannah Trefgarne
Editorial assistant: Charlotte Meredith
Production editor: Rachel Burrows
Copyeditor: Christine Bitten
Proofreader: Bryan Campbell
Indexer: Adam Pozner
Marketing manager: Camille Richmond
Cover design: Shaun Mercier
Typeset by: C&M Digitals (P) Ltd, Chennai, India

ISBN 978-1-4462-9665-3
ISBN 978-1-4462-9666-0 (pbk)

This book is dedicated to my amazingly tolerant family and friends for their combination of encouragement, patience and good humour

CONTENTS

ABOUT THE AUTHOR

Since completing her training as a mental health nurse in 1987, Kirsten has spent over 20 years working as a counsellor, lecturer in counselling and supervisor within the NHS, education, private practice and voluntary sectors. In addition to this, she works as an SQA Appointee in the role of External Verifier for counselling qualifications. Kirsten's published work includes *Challenges in Counselling: Counselling Students*, (2013, Hodder) and *Becoming a Counsellor: A Student Companion* (2011, Sage). Her areas of interest include counselling students, counselling training and working with addiction.

ACKNOWLEDGEMENTS

There are several people I would like to thank for their support during the research, compilation and writing of this book. To begin with, a massive thank you to Andrew Reeves for his unfailing support, wisdom and editing wizardry; the team at Sage for their tolerance and experience; Christine Bitten for her keen eye and sound suggestions; and Andy, for allowing me to impose on his reading habits.

Thanks also to Jim Carmichael for his generosity of time to share his considerable knowledge on the philosophy and history of ethics. And thank you to David MacAllan, Laura Buchanan, Rosemary Stewart and Lynn Taylor for adopting an interested expression and not wandering off when I started talking about ethical dilemmas in the snug.

Last, but not least, a quiet but incredibly grateful 'thank you' to all my clients, students, supervisor (and a couple of random strangers) who have contributed in more ways than they can ever know!

WHAT ARE BOUNDARIES?

Before progressing to the finer detail of boundaried therapeutic work, it is helpful to clarify some of the specific meanings within the context of counselling. Considering what we mean by the term 'boundaries' in counselling should help, in addition to considering how such boundaries can be used as a vehicle for therapeutic change. With so many models of therapy being practised, we also need to explore the impact that our theoretical orientation can have on the contracting process. We will also consider a range of possible alternatives for managing our boundaries. Within this chapter we will be considering the challenges and benefits that working within safe boundaries can provide; to do that however, we first need to clarify exactly what we mean by boundaries within professional counselling relationships.

COUNSELLING AND THE VERY NATURE OF COUNSELLING

There are probably hundreds of explanations of the activity of counselling but the BACP define counselling as being:

> ... time set aside by you and the therapist to look at what has brought you to therapy. This might include talking about life events (past and present), feelings, emotions, relationships, ways of thinking and patterns of behaviour. The therapist will do their best to help you to look at your issues, and to identify the right course of action for you, either to help you resolve your difficulties or help you find ways of coping. Talking about these things may take time, and will not necessarily all be included in one session.

This definition introduces several notions: that of the breadth of potential content a client might wish to discuss; the counsellor's role in facilitating progress; that the process can take differing lengths of time for different people; and that the process is divided into sessions. There are several aspects of this process that might be confusing for a new client who hasn't experienced counselling before; an honest discussion between client and counsellor about the process will start the relationship on a more even footing, clarify any expectations or allay any fears. By framing boundaries in this way, it helps us view them as a positive aspect of the relationship that provides a shared safety and security, as opposed to negative restrictions or rules which is how they may be considered within other contexts.

WHAT WE MEAN BY BOUNDARIES

If we are working with a client new to counselling however, much as we try to avoid it there is an instant imbalance of power within the relationship. The counsellor will have expectations based on their own personal and professional experience, while the client's expectations may be based on a different range of external sources. It is possible that a new client may expect a counsellor to give them answers, or at least guidance, whereas the counsellor's way of working may never involve such a directive approach. This illustrates the potential for client and counsellor to be approaching the sessions, content and process from very different perspectives.

To avoid this, we aim to simultaneously reduce differences in expectation, or at least acknowledge those differences, while increasing the equality within the relationship. It is ethically important during the first meeting for a counsellor to explain their counselling process and discuss the aim or purpose of their service with every client. An integral aspect of this is to agree the external and internal conditions that they will both adhere to in developing a working contract. This discussion takes place before any therapeutic work begins and is an opportunity for both parties to question and clarify the details of what will take place during their time working together.

To be clear, when we talk of boundaries we are talking of:

- the rules, guidelines and safe margins that we work within to ensure the maximum security for a client and counsellor
- the best possible conditions for therapeutic development
- a shared agreement of the limits of the relationship.

A BACP factsheet providing guidance on the area of professional issues explains them as '... *maintain(ing) clear standards of therapy and protect(ing) you from poor or unethical practice*' (Kent, 2012). By clarifying the limits of the relationship with our client, it allows us to adopt a role more akin to that of facilitator, as opposed to a manager or expert. It also encourages an increase in shared trust, as both client and counsellor discuss, agree and implement the boundaries to their meetings. This level of transparency adds to the culture of equality and is intended for the client to feel sufficiently safe to be as open, honest and emotionally vulnerable as might be required. The client also needs to be confident that the counsellor can be trusted to value and safeguard that information. Because of this, some boundaries are non-negotiable, such as issues surrounding confidentiality or venue, which are informed by legislation, policies, organisations and ethical frameworks.

There are many types of boundaries, many of which we shall visit later, but they include the number, regularity and length of sessions, referral, orientation, setting, environment, ethics, supervision and cost. The management of risk or a safe plan may also be included within this list so the client is aware of a course of action if they experience a crisis when not in the counselling session. Due to the uniqueness and dynamics of counselling, none of these aspects are clear cut, as they are influenced by a range of internal and external considerations. These considerations are many and varied but can include the setting the counselling is taking place in, the theoretical orientation of the counsellor, the cultural norms of the client and ethical guidelines.

These external influences can introduce an initial source of inequality within the relationship if a client is unaware of factors, such as funding or ethical guidelines. In addition to this, some boundaries are enforced by other external bodies, such as indemnity insurance providers and organisational policies and procedures, so are far less flexible. As a counsellor, we have a responsibility to discuss and explain the governing influences behind certain requirements so the client can understand the reasoning behind such boundaries. For example, a client travelling a long way to attend and wishing their sessions to be longer than the usual therapeutic hour may lead to a negotiation process that might include explaining the policy of the service in such circumstances, what research informs us regarding therapeutic benefit in relation to session length, diary commitments and of course, personal preference. The outcome is then up to both client and counsellor to agree based on the shared information.

MAKING USE OF BOUNDARIES AS A VEHICLE FOR THERAPEUTIC CHANGE

The sharing of information regarding boundaries contributes towards a client's increased empowerment; this is a key aspect of the therapeutic relationship. The content of the counselling sessions can impact upon the client beyond the realm of the session and into the rest of the week, if not longer. Giving the client a voice, highlighting their choices and taking time to hear their contribution might be an experience that doesn't happen often in other aspects of their life. Engaging with our client as a valued equal can lay down a foundation of warmth, acceptance and trust, creating important preparation for a successful therapeutic relationship.

The negotiation process during the contracting session is a highly successful method of clarifying the role of counselling and encouraging the client to shape their environment within certain parameters, while discussing their own expectations and requirements. Shifting the balance so that the client shares in the responsibility of establishing a foundation for change gives the client permission and space to test their ability to take control of some aspects, as well as sharing how they feel regarding others. For many clients control, or the lack of it, is a core issue when attending counselling; a careful and kind dialogue can encourage the client to value their input from the very first meeting. This real demonstration of interest and care for the client is setting a precedent for the dynamics within the relationship. It is putting Rogers' 'organismic valuing into practice' (Rogers, 1964: 160–167).

Here is an example of a trainee counsellor's introduction to agreeing boundaries in which Anne remembers her trepidation when starting her Introduction to Counselling course:

'I remember how nervous I felt on my first day. I had never done anything like this before and had no idea what to expect. After my interview several months earlier I was given a course handbook which contained a reading list and sections on how to submit assessments and how to contact tutors but nothing to prepare me for who I was going to meet or how I would feel. When I walked into the classroom my first reaction was that I was relieved to see that I wasn't the oldest on the course which I realised had been a worry. It was on our second day that we sat in a circle and agreed class rules which we all signed and was put on the wall. It was quite detailed and included things like turning phones off, confidentiality, respect and being honest but kind to each other. Just by sharing that task as a group it gave me a reason to speak to others and was my first experience of how we might work as a group.'

Anne's experience illustrates how a contracting session, whether it be in a group or a one-to-one session, can break the ice and encourage a discussion on an equal footing. Both student and tutor, or client and counsellor, are placed in a position of empowerment when they are both given a voice. A similar process takes place within other counselling environments, such as group therapy, couple and family therapy, as well as individual counselling sessions. Focusing on some of the less flexible external and organisational procedures can be a gentle way to start a new relationship, particularly one that will be moving away from the external and concentrating more on internal processes in the future. For it to be part of the therapeutic process, formal contracting can be approached in a friendly and helpful manner to introduce the client to a professional way of working, and to lessen any concerns regarding what can be seen by some as a confusing and secretive activity.

Iain had a similar experience, feeling nervous and trepidatious, but on starting his placement was very positive about the contracting process when reflecting on it with his supervisor.

'I was quite nervous before my first session. I had received my readiness to practise statement from my course tutor but as I was waiting for my first client to arrive, I didn't feel ready. The service I was working for had a written contract that was very clear about the areas that could be negotiated and I used that as the basis for our session. As it turned out, my client was new to counselling too so didn't have any previous experience to refer to as a comparison. We worked through the sections together and I was surprised that it took so long. I encouraged her to expand on her thoughts about each separate aspect and found out a lot about her which is how we started. I wasn't as clear as I thought I'd be about where the contracting ended and where the counselling began.'

THE IMPACT OF EXTERNAL ASPECTS ON BOUNDARIES

The psychological theory that underpins our practice will influence not just the way we approach contracting but also how we come to agreements in future therapy. This relationship between our model of therapy and working with boundaries is discussed in more depth in Chapter 9 but can be summarised thus. If we are working with a more directive theoretical orientation, the contents of the contract may be slightly less negotiable. If we are working with a less directive approach we may be comfortable negotiating much of the content. By this I mean, we must demonstrate a professional flexibility that caters for not just the needs of our client, but also blends the requirements of the organisation we work within and our own value base. This blended approach shows us how the contracting process is an integral part of the counselling relationship and encourages the client to experience the underpinning ethos of our relationship rather than an isolated process.

Consider this example:

> Damien works as a counsellor within an addiction service. His core training is person-centred but the organisation he works for requires him to include an aspect of education in his sessions. This means Damien is expected to demonstrate that he is offering relevant information about the effects of addiction to his clients. The service also encourages all clients to attend their 12-step programme. In the evenings Damien rents an office and maintains a small private practice. He sees four clients a week and has written his own policies and procedures based on his person-centred way of being. His private clients are all self-funding so Damien has far more freedom regarding the management of his service.

Here we can see that the policies of this organisation and their general ethos impact quite significantly on Damien's practice during the day. For continuity throughout the addiction service, all counsellors working there are required to include information giving and an awareness of the 12-step programme, in addition to their therapeutic approach. The contracting, therefore, is not completely in the hands of Damien and his clients, but heavily influenced by the organisational requirements that, in turn, may well come from influential funding bodies. For Damien to work successfully for this service, his person-centred approach will have to underpin his practice in a way that can accommodate the less flexible aspects of the contracting. However, in his private work, he is able to practise with more freedom and a far greater sense of autonomy.

This example highlights the constraints and benefits of a different sector.

Joanne is a CBT practitioner employed by the NHS. So far she has found very little conflict between her structured therapeutic work and the boundaries determined by the organisation. She feels that the rigidity of the medical routine (appointment system, venue, statutory funding, etc.) have worked to reinforce her counselling process. During her sessions, she focuses on reinforcing positive behaviours and the repetition of successful change so both the regularity and formality of the setting are very much part of the process. Joanne feels that the setting unconsciously reinforces how she (and the wider health service) is taking the client and the therapeutic process seriously.

As we can see from these examples of Damien and Joanne, in addition to our underpinning theoretical model, the setting we are based in can also impact upon our boundaries. Examples can include working within a statutory service, such as the NHS, social work department, schools or prisons, where there are nationally and locally developed policies and procedures guiding our working practices, whether relating to counselling or to the wider organisation and its culture. The frustrations that can accompany this therapeutic/employee tension will be explored within Chapter 8.

We have already identified that being based within the voluntary sector can shape our working practices, but let's look at the practicalities and the impact that these can have on our client. Consider the following example of working with a client within a drug rehabilitation service.

This was Gerry's third engagement with a rehabilitation service. Initially he had been referred to the local Community Addiction Team but relapsed twice. Several months later he approached a local organisation with a drop-in service on the recommendation of a friend. Gerry felt quite jaded by his past experiences and focused on what

(Continued)

(Continued)

he viewed as his previous failures. On his first meeting with his new counsellor Sonia, he was cautious, suspicious and very guarded. He had learned to be resistant to being told what to do by others but at the same time didn't trust his own coping strategies. This resulted in Gerry simultaneously distrusting both himself and those helping him. Sonia had worked in the centre for five years and was aware of the inner turmoil that new clients could experience.

What might Sonia do in that first meeting to engage with Gerry and develop an equitable relationship?

Although not a definitive checklist, these are some possible areas that can be used to start to build a positive relationship.

- Ask Gerry to define his aims and ultimate goal
- Clearly explain her role as a counsellor and the services the organisation can provide
- Invite Gerry to recognise what didn't work in his previous endeavours
- Encourage Gerry to identify his strengths
- Demonstrate to Gerry that he is at the centre of his recovery by listening to his viewpoint
- Embedding his values within the initial contract
- Ensuring that time is spent negotiating the more flexible boundaries to demonstrate to Gerry that his opinion counts.

By implementing these steps, Sonia provides a structure for the therapy that has its foundation in Gerry's previous experiences. It also communicates to Gerry that he is central to the process and that his contribution can help mould the counselling and their future relationship. This, in turn, communicates a sharing of power intended to challenge Gerry's lack of faith in his own coping strategies in a manner that demonstrates this is an equitable process designed to establish trust.

POSSIBLE ALTERNATIVES FOR MANAGING BOUNDARIES

Following the initial agreement or contracting session, boundaries need to be re-visited and managed to ensure that they are being adhered to, but also that they are working as hoped. When more than one client is involved, such as in couples, family or group counselling, there is a greater requirement to ensure that all parties are clear on what will take place and that everyone has been given an equal opportunity to contribute. This may involve explaining and agreeing factors several times in a range of ways if our clients are of different ages or have varying levels of understanding to each other. It is the counsellor's responsibility to clarify all aspects of the agreement and check that the client is aware and comfortable with the content. It might be helpful to use examples to illustrate the implications of particular parameters of the sessions and relationship, particularly when explaining our theoretical orientation or therapeutic process. Just as each client is a unique individual, so is the dynamic of our interactions with them. Although we can have our own personal and professional expectations of what might take place, it is impossible to predict. Therefore, we have to be sufficiently prepared for, and sufficiently flexible to deal with, any occurrence that might arise.

Here are some of the situations that might occur within sessions. What might be done in each of these situations to manage our original agreement?

(a) A client consciously or unconsciously ignoring the end of the session and wishing to continue.
(b) A client's mobile phone ringing.
(c) A client becoming angry and walking out.
(d) A client describing events in detail but completely resistant to discussing their feelings.
(e) A client disclosing abuse.
(f) A client you suspect is avoiding paying.
(g) A client admitting that they are attracted to us.
(h) One client dominating the session in couples' counselling.
(i) Clients in a group session talking over each other.
(j) A client wanting to end their sessions as they are finding it too upsetting.

There are no definite answers to any of these examples as so many factors influence each situation. One solution doesn't fit all, but rather there are a range of possible alternatives for responding when our boundaries are challenged. There are also many strategies we can put in place to manage both our sessions and our relationship which we will look at further in Chapter 8 using these same examples. As previously mentioned, the combination of flexibility and care is crucial if we are to communicate to our client that this is an equitable relationship.

The ability to see the bigger picture, consider the background of the current situation and respond in a manner that avoids impulsive, knee-jerk reactions and be guided by our theoretical approach, are skills that might take time to develop, but are crucial in our ability to maintain boundaries in a professional and appropriate manner. Clients can knowingly or unknowingly try to manipulate us into collusion, agreement or advice giving, so we need to remain vigilant about our responses, what they might mean to the client, and any impact they might have on the development of the therapeutic alliance. We can work with our supervisor to have strategies in place that we are comfortable using to support our client. We are aiming to develop methods that maintain the therapeutic connection but, at the same time, respond in a manner that remains within the agreed limits of our relationship. This can be challenging to say the least, particularly if you are unprepared, but the most important tool in this case is transparency. Maintaining our boundaries can become an integral part of the therapeutic process if we remain honest and open to encourage self-awareness and insight. If a client challenges their boundaries we shouldn't just highlight it, but make it part of our session. The use of immediacy in this way can help move the session forward. It demonstrates that we are aware of what is taking place, we feel that it is relevant and that we are unafraid to challenge our client. The challenge may be gentle as in the case of examples (g) or (j) above or more direct in the case of examples (a) and (f).

The approach to, and method of, managing boundaries is covered within our core counselling training and we know can vary depending on which theoretical orientation we are working within. For example, a CBT therapist may be more pragmatic in their approach, employing available evidence, direct challenge and may develop tools specifically to work with that particular client. This may differ considerably from the approach of a person-centred counsellor who may implement the core conditions to formulate a less direct challenge. The key is to remain aware of the context and implications of any challenge and to respond in a manner appropriate to both the boundary that is being tested and our own modality.

What this means on a practical level is that we

- refer back to our initial contract
- pre-empt some of the situations and strategise with our supervisor
- include guidelines within a service leaflet (such as payment methods, session length, complaints procedure)
- give a copy of the contract to clients before they engage with the service.

Although not mandatory, there are numerous situations where providing a leaflet or signed contract outlining our service significantly helps reduce the incidences of boundary confusion. An example of this is if we work with children and young people, or clients at risk where informed consent needs to be sought (this will be discussed further in Chapter 3). Having an explanatory leaflet or information on a website can also reinforce the transparency of the service by including an overview of the general process. It is often useful to view the information that other services provide to help formulate an appropriate document for your own service. There are many available online, but this is an example of information provided on a website for a student counselling service:

What do we do?

Counselling is an opportunity to talk to a trained professional who can help us work out how to deal with our personal problems. These can include long-standing issues and short-term crises. Our counselling service offers free, private counselling to all students currently enrolled at the college. We provide friendly, private support to students who wish help with any difficulties they may be experiencing. Talking through your problems can help to improve your wellbeing and impact positively on your studying. It may be beneficial to speak to someone outside your immediate group of family, friends and tutors. For more details, watch the short BACP film on the Counselling Service page on the college website.

What problems do students see a counsellor about?

You can approach a counsellor with any personal problem. Problems arising from a variety of issues such as:

1. trouble with family and friends
2. feelings resulting from an event such as bereavement or trauma
3. difficulties adjusting to life as a student
4. living away from home
5. addiction
6. stress
7. anxiety
8. low mood.

Counsellors can also help you access assistance from an outside specialist agency if you would find that helpful. The counselling service will not be able to assist with practical issues such as funding, housing, childcare or benefits.

(Continued)

(Continued)

Will anyone know if i attend counselling?

No, not even your course tutor or lecturers unless you specifically request it. The counselling service guarantees privacy to all students. The counselling rooms are anonymous and used by different services so not identifiable to those passing by. Students of all ages, backgrounds, gender, full or part-time and distance learners can make use of the counselling service.

How much time will it take up?

As a guideline, each session lasts for 50 minutes. The frequency of the visits is usually weekly but depends upon what you and your counsellor agree is appropriate. You are requested to make counselling appointments for a time when you are not timetabled to be in class. If you are unable to attend your appointment, please contact your counsellor with at least 24 hours' notice to cancel your session.

How much does it cost?

There is no charge for students attending counselling as the service is funded by the college.

Does the counsellor take notes?

Yes, all our counsellors take notes at the end of each session which are stored securely within the college. You are able to ask your counsellor to see these at any time.

How do you make an appointment?

If you would like to access counselling, you can either book a session on the Student Intranet, College App or you can approach your Student Advice Team. Counselling can be accessed at any of the campuses, not only the campus you are currently attending. When necessary we also accept external referrals from GPs, Social Workers, NHS and courts. Please be aware that referrals from members of staff are not usually supported.

The information is designed to outline the overarching boundaries of the service and clarify those aspects that are not flexible. The time of sessions is stipulated, but the venue isn't. To have a majority of inflexible boundaries can be demanding and testing. Those that are pre-fixed due to external circumstances might include the policies and procedures of the service, or the confines of the setting you are working within. Restrictions might include cost, number of sessions (e.g. eight if referred from GP or the maximum offered within service), the available room to work in, how often we can meet with our client, etc. Having the fixed and negotiable boundaries contained with a leaflet, written contract, email or website can be particularly helpful for a client to receive in advance to help them decide whether the service you offer is likely to meet their needs. Such clarity clearly meets the BACP (2015) ethical guidelines on commitment to clients:

4. Build an appropriate relationship with clients by:

   a. Communicating clearly what clients have a right to expect from us.
   b. Communicating any benefits, costs and commitments that clients may reasonably expect.
   c. Respecting the boundaries between our work with clients and what lies outside that work.
   d. Not exploiting or abusing clients.
   e. Listening out for how clients experience our working together.

AREAS OF CONCERN AND POTENTIAL CHALLENGES

Although the majority might prefer a more passive role in the process, reaching an agreement with clients in a way that meets both their expectations and our professional requirements can be a daunting prospect. This isn't only regarding possible challenges, but also from encouraging clients to feel sufficiently empowered to contribute from a position of understanding. Some counsellors, particularly when first starting out, find the process a source of tension. However, if a new client has read through our available marketing literature and made an informed decision to attend, they are less likely to be resistant to engagement.

Whilst plenty of time was hopefully spent within your training considering the range of boundaries in counselling practice, this should be balanced with considering the impact that each can have on the counsellor, the client and the alliance. To begin with, no amount of preparation in a classroom setting can totally remove all anxieties when being faced with a new client, and neither should it. The key to reducing potential barriers to a smooth working relationship with our clients is to employ a combination of clarity, flexibility, transparency and negotiation. This initial process can have a profound impact upon clients and can be for reasons we may not be aware of. Because of this, it is beneficial for all involved to encourage questions not just during the first meeting but throughout the time working together.

In addition to the initial process, there are other, more specific areas of concern that many counsellors experience at any point in their career. The following are just a few examples that have arisen during sessions with both new and experienced supervisees:

1. I'm not sure what the professional guidelines recommend.
2. What evidence are my decisions based on?
3. What am I legally required to offer?
4. How do I keep safe?
5. How do I keep my client safe?
6. What if there is a complaint about me?
7. How do I know that what we're doing is working?
8. Is the environment conducive to our working together?
9. How do I decide what to charge?

The good news is that as long as we can be clear about where our concern lies, it is considerably easier to find a solution that we are comfortable with. Whether this comes from our supervisor, our professional guidelines, course tutor (if in training), our colleagues, professional journal, additional reading, CPD or our line manager. The list isn't exhaustive but does highlight how many resources we have available to us when we reach a point of uncertainty. Even if none of these concerns have cropped up in your counselling work, having a strategy in place to face concerns should they occur is part of our professional preparation. If this is an area of concern for you, the above list can be used as a basic framework to reflect on in supervision. We should be identifying gaps in our knowledge and confidence so that we feel more prepared should an anxiety arise in future. Then we are making sure that our supervision isn't just reflective, but also strategic and preparatory too, reinforcing our own self-care.

As well as potential concerns regarding our professional practice, there are also uncomfortable or unexpected situations that can arise from our client. Depending upon how prepared we feel, in some instances these may be viewed as potential challenges to a counsellor. These might include:

1. A client disagreeing.
2. A client referring to previous experience that was different (better or worse).
3. External restraints such as working within educational setting.
4. Counsellor's lack of confidence.
5. Counsellor's fear of forgetting something.
6. A client might not feel sufficiently confident to contribute.
7. A very experienced and confident client working with a new and inexperienced counsellor.

8. A client being resistant to boundaries, interpreting them as being told what to do.
9. A client being distrustful.

The one aspect these all have in common is that they might suggest powerlessness but in the opposite way to that often assumed. Rather than the client feeling at a disadvantage, here the counsellor might feel that the equality in the alliance is compromised or fractured; that the client has adopted a challenging or controlling position and the imbalance of power has them at a disadvantage. This illustrates how the distribution and perception of power can distort the relationship and will be considered in the next chapter using these same examples.

Questions for reflection

Here are some additional questions for personal reflection, which you might take to clinical supervision. You might also discuss them with colleagues in relation to your organisation's current boundaries. More ideas for reflecting on the professional aspects of our boundaries are covered in Chapter 3. Allocating development time to consider alternative responses and approaches might raise awareness of any areas you need to clarify. Avoid focusing just on counselling situations but consider your relationship with boundaries in other areas of your life.

1. What are my thoughts about rules in general?
2. How do I respond when I'm governed by rules?
3. Which therapeutic boundaries am I most comfortable with?
4. Why is this?
5. Which boundaries am I least comfortable with, and why?

If, in answering these questions you have identified any fears, uncertainties or worries, make a record of them and discuss them at your next supervision session. A feeling of resistance or discomfort with aspects of the contracting agreement may well be unintentionally communicated to your client. We are aiming to blend our professional theoretical and ethical grounding with our personal moral stance. Being comfortable and confident with the way in which we conduct our contracting lays a solid foundation for any future therapeutic work together.

Chapter summary

This chapter has given us a basis for considering our relationship with boundaries and hopefully it has also identified any areas for development. The flexibility and negotiation of boundaries isn't just between the counsellor and client but also between the counsellor and organisation or company they work with. Boundaries should be a constant work in progress that reflect developments and changes in law, professional guidelines, research findings and feedback from those using our service. To balance that, we must ensure that our way of working is also compatible with our own values and moral compass.

FURTHER READING

Corey, G., Corey M.S., & Corey, C. (2015). *Issues and ethics in the helping professions* (9th edn). Boston, MA: Brooks Cole.

Hartmann, E. (1997). The concept of boundaries in counselling and psychotherapy. *British Journal of Guidance & Counselling, 25*(2), 147–162.

Knox, R., & Cooper, M. (2015). *The therapeutic relationship in counselling and psychotherapy*. London: Sage.

DEFINING ETHICS, POWER AND RESPONSIBILITY

This chapter will focus on core terminology and some fundamental questions relating to why boundaries are underpinned by ethics, as well as why we should be alert to any potential power imbalance. Using examples, we will reflect on any subsequent impact this might have on our therapeutic alliance. Raising awareness and identifying any evidence of imbalance will then help us determine the therapist's power and responsibilities when working with boundaries. Our current practice is heavily influenced by the successful and less successful practices of counsellors over the years, so the historical context to the development of thinking in this area is relevant. In the past, talking therapies were less monitored, researched and accessible and practitioners were not guided by the ethical frameworks and legal parameters that we work within now. Raising awareness of the impact that underpinning theoretical orientations can have, as well as cultural differences, should help us shape an equitable and accessible service. Much of this reflection will touch on the relationship between our boundary management and our perceived or actual power and responsibility.

CORE TERMINOLOGY

By now it may have become apparent that the terms 'ethics' and 'morals' are used regularly within counselling training and settings. No-one is expecting us to be an expert in law or philosophy, but we are expected to have a working understanding of how their meaning and application helps us to understand the influences underpinning the formulation of our contracts with clients. Professional ethics and our own personal morals are also a core aspect of our reflective practice. Often, the terms are used interchangeably but they refer to subtly different aspects of our beliefs, attitudes and behaviours.

On a very simple level ethics is the science of morals and a philosophical practice. They are principles or guidelines that underpin our choices and tend to be shared within professions, societies and cultures as rules for good behaviour. Morals however, are more personal and determine how each of us puts ethics into practice in our own way. They can be influenced by our upbringing, culture and experiences, so are more subjective. Together with other conditions, such as the law and organisational procedures, ethical guidelines combined with our own moral judgments influence how we respond to a dilemma.

Consider the following scenario:

> John is a new client attending your practice. He tells you during your first meeting that he has chosen to make an appointment with you as you have counselled his wife Anne and she recommended you.

Can you identify any ethical considerations in this situation? How might you respond in a manner that sits comfortably with your personal morals?

There may be several areas you might consider:

- Are you still working with Anne?
- Will you be able to separate any of John's session content that involves her?
- What if Anne requests further sessions in the future?

These may be fairly straightforward questions and can be discussed with your counselling supervisor, but would you feel differently if Anne had talked about how John abused her? Or if John asked for a joint session with both of them present? Or if Anne had talked at length of her affair? In this situation it is helpful to consider the range of influences on our professional judgment making. These include our legal obligations, the policies and procedures of the organisation we are working for (even if that is in private practice), the ethical framework of our professional body, our own moral compass and any previous experiences we may have had that can help guide us.

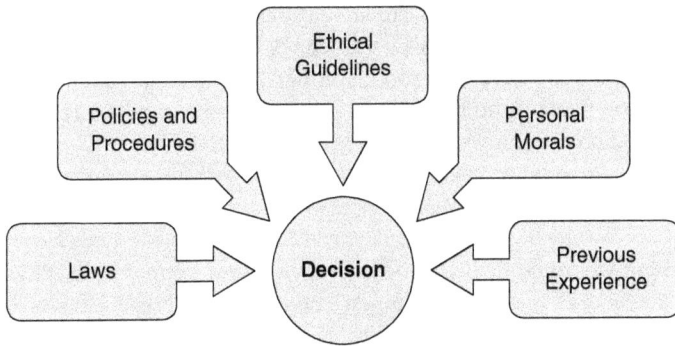

Figure 2.1

These are in addition to our professional principles, which include being trustworthy at all times, being able to combine collaborative working in supervision with our own self-governance, working in a manner that is 'good', ensuring that we do no harm, our choices and behaviours are fair and just and that we behave with honour and dignity.

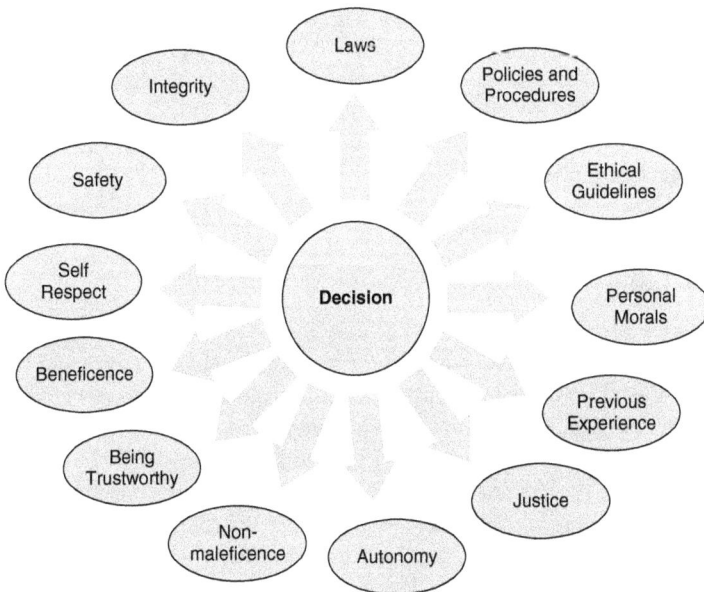

Figure 2.2

A common tension that can arise in relation to this process is the way we understand our ethical guidelines. There are counsellors who raise the issue of a professional conflict between the content being either too fixed or too flexible. For example, some, particularly newly qualified counsellors, would prefer a prescriptive format that clearly outlines set rules to follow in a range of situations. If this were the case, the immediate consequence would be that our options and choices would be reduced and our ability for professional decision making would be denied. The inference would be that both we as a sector, and as individuals, couldn't be trusted to make safe choices based on our clients' needs. Ethical guidelines would become prescriptive ethical rules and would challenge the assumption that our clients are unique individuals.

Replacing a framework with a rule book would also assume that all situations can be approached in the same way. As we work in a profession that emphasises the individuality of people, it is hard to ally that with dictating how everyone should act in a given situation. When it comes to situations of risk where safety is paramount, the law provides parameters which are flexible in some areas and prescriptive in others. As a result of this, the current process is far more holistic, flexible and supports decisions being made to measure for each client. But as Davies (2015: 6) identifies, *'Ethical decision making also involves consultation with peers and colleagues or with supervisors. It involves gathering evidence from research to decide how best to apply professional ethical code values and principles in practice.'* This clearly illustrates how our practice is not dictated by inflexible rules, but is rather a reflexive process that is informed by a range of influences and designed specifically for each and every client.

WHY ARE BOUNDARIES UNDERPINNED BY ETHICS?

The easiest way to understand the relationship between ethics and the boundaries we make in a contract is to imagine what sessions would be like without them; if our decision-making process was purely arbitrary. Without guidelines for safe practice, clients would no longer be able to rely on our professionalism and it would become very challenging to justify our working practice. Essentially, there would be a significant risk to both counsellor and client. If we find making ethical decisions challenging with all the guidance available to us now, imagine how much harder it would be with nowhere to turn for advice. However, rather than boundaries all being completely fixed or flexible, we are trained to maintain a balance between being autonomous practitioners and part of a safe and reflective profession. Because of that, our professional training is designed to prepare us for finding ourselves in situations with clients where we are unsure of our next step. This ensures we are equipped with the skills to reflect on any situation that occurs within the counselling room and make an informed decision regarding our next step.

Although there to guide us, no professional ethical framework will be completely prescriptive but, rather, provide a context or agenda on which to base our choices and decisions. As part of that process we should develop a strategy for approaching challenges that allows us to consider and be influenced by that context, but also marry it with our value base, our professional practice, our organisational ethos and current legislation. It also helps to contextualise the process by including different perspectives: the history of the situation, how it presents today and how any decisions may impact on the future.

As examples, consider basic boundaries such as confidentiality and disclosure, session length and cost. The limits of these may be predetermined by our organisation, but the client wouldn't know that unless it had been shared, either in marketing literature or during the contracting session. Until that point, the counsellor would hold the power of knowledge simply by being aware of the confidentiality policy, the 50-minute 'therapeutic hour' and the cost of sessions. However, this imbalance becomes less straightforward when issues arise that challenge our working norms. As Reamer (2013: 2) explains, '*Boundary issues arise when human service professionals encounter actual or potential conflicts between their professional duties and their social, sexual, religious, collegial or business relationships.*'

Here are some examples that highlight the impact that such conflict can have on our dialogue surrounding boundaries.

Question: Florence attends her first session with you in the addiction service where you work. She requests guaranteed 100% confidentiality as she is terrified of her family finding out that she is attending. How would you discuss the organisation's confidentiality policy with her?

Florence may not be aware that counsellors respect confidentiality up to a point that is determined by law. By allowing her to read the Service's confidentiality policy, she can make an informed decision as to whether this meets her needs. Further discussion on this can be found in Chapter 4.

Question: You are in private practice and have a session with a new client. When Joe attends, he explains that as he lives a three-hour drive away and as this is the closest counselling service to his home, he would prefer a fortnightly two-hour session which would be considerably more convenient. How do you feel about this? What would you do?

This is an area where, for some counselling services, there may be increased flexibility, although adjustments to working practice should be carefully considered, discussed with your line manager and clinical supervisor and be agreed by all concerned. Other services might refuse, arguing that concentration can wane during longer sessions.

Question: You are explaining to Jack, a new client that you charge £45 per session but he says that he's currently unemployed and can't afford that much. What is your response?

You may have a payment system, such as a sliding scale according to what clients can afford, or are comfortable with clients donating what they can afford – consequently this might not be so much of an issue. However, if you are in private practice and have to pay overheads, such as room rental, this situation isn't so clear-cut. It is important to have a strategy in place for such situations. A simple solution is to send all new clients an overview of your service before the first session so that they are aware of the practical details and can make an informed decision based on the content. Of course, this can include details of a sliding scale of payment if that is your choice.

All three of these examples illustrate how some issues we encounter can be very basic and easily accommodated. Others however can be far less straightforward and require further clarification as to what we can and can't adapt. At this point we should be considering the three main influences on our professional decision making and the tensions that such a process can uncover.

Flexibility and transparency are the key to the successful negotiation of safe limits and, how we structure our work now, is the result of many years of reflective practice, research and developments within the law. Today, what we accept as professional working practices have altered significantly since the first talking therapies. It is widely accepted that Sigmund Freud had, by today's standards, rather more 'flexible' boundaries: he sent

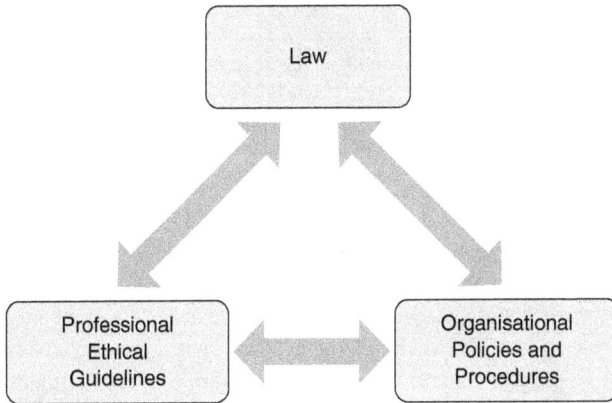

Figure 2.3

postcards to clients, lent them his books and gave them presents. His dogs were often present during sessions and he is known to have discussed his own family with clients and even joined his clients for meals on holiday. He also analysed his own daughter. Such behaviours now would have cause to be highly criticised if a counsellor's professional life and social life were so overlapped. Without recognising and respecting the boundary between the professional relationship and the personal relationship, such informal exchanges could impact upon trust, confidentiality and a lack of rigour when monitoring progress. The equivalent would be meeting your family doctor socially and taking the opportunity to discuss personal health matters.

WHAT IS THE POTENTIAL POWER IMBALANCE?

Initially, when we focus on power within the therapy room it is easy to assume that the counsellor has all the power: they are within their own environment, this is not their first client and know what to expect. However, the counsellor's area of knowledge and experience will form only a small part of the therapeutic relationship. The client, by definition a stranger, is attending to discuss themselves and their world of which the counsellor knows either nothing or very little. Therefore, from the first meeting there will be areas that are known and areas that are not known to either party.

As a reflective process, it can be useful to apply our working practices to a Johari window model (Luft & Ingham, 1955) as a method of identifying what is known and what is not to both the client and the counsellor

Table 2.1 *Applying the Johari window to counselling*

Open area known to counsellor and client	Blind spot known by client but not by counsellor
Hidden area known by counsellor but not by client	Unknown to both counsellor and client

within the relationship. It can provide a clear framework for viewing the holistic relationship and highlighting any potential power imbalance.

The open area which is known to both self and others will include all aspects of the counselling sessions that are known equally by counsellor and client. This is the element of the working relationship that you are hoping to expand. In an ideal situation, our marketing materials, leaflets, printed contract and open discussions should place as much information in this quadrant as possible. This is the section that can reduce a client's anxiety with regard to attending counselling and the possible aims and outcomes.

Within the hidden area known by self (counsellor) and not by others (client), we might consider aspects of the counselling relationship that we, as counsellors, are aware of but our client might not be. By openly encouraging questions and the sharing of concerns, we should be able to move content from this quadrant into the shared knowledge section. There might be practical changes we can make which might include where is the clock placed and who can see it? At the end of the session, do you say 'we have to end now' or have an alternative method to indicate the session is ending? Are your certificates on view? Is there an exchange of money at the end of the session? These are examples of some of the choices we may take for granted but can shift the power balance in favour of the counsellor, whilst being intimidating for the client. It can be difficult to both reassure your client that you are well qualified but at the same time not intimidate them by appearing to be an expert with all the answers.

David's situation illustrates a possible situation where the inequality is contextualised and touches directly on the client's issue for attending.

> David has been attending counselling for three sessions due to withdrawing from his university course as a result of his high anxiety levels. He is feeling rather uncomfortable as when he sits down, the wall opposite has numerous framed certificates on it. He finds himself feeling slightly jealous of the counsellor and isn't able to consider them as an equal.

The blind spot known by other (client) but not by self (counsellor) refers to the client's world: their hopes, expectations and experiences. This sector relates to the content of the counselling sessions as well as the client's understanding of the counselling process. The majority of time together will be spent in this section covering the client's reason for attending, their thoughts, feelings, relationships, hopes and fears. It takes great strength by the client to make themselves vulnerable and trust a counsellor with personal content that the counsellor didn't previously know. As sessions progress, this sector should shrink, moving content over to the open area but only as far as the client wishes. This is where they are very much in control.

Jacky's experience includes just this; a situation that she feels is very private and personal and has yet to share with anyone else.

> Jacky has been referred to counselling by her employer. She is tearful and has had a high level of absences recently although is adamant that nothing is wrong. Two months ago whilst shopping, Jacky caught sight of her uncle who she hadn't seen since she was twelve years old. She understood that he was still in prison for sexually abusing herself and her sister. Since then she hasn't been able to think about anything else.

Finally, the section that is unknown to self and others encapsulates the relationship and dynamic between both client and counsellor. It is the unknown and in relation to boundaries, highlights any aspects that will develop, emerge and require to be faced during the length of the therapeutic relationship. Issues relating to transference, dependency and progress will require identification, discussion and negotiation so that both parties are comfortable with developments and change. Working with the unknown is how we challenge ourselves professionally, identify areas for further development and mature as counsellors.

> Today, Dominic disclosed in his counselling session that he has started wearing his wife's tights when he is alone at home. This is not a situation you have worked with before and are initially unsure of how to respond.

These three situations offer examples of several areas in which the counsellor may disempower the client; the sensitivity in which we handle disclosed information will either encourage or discourage the client and, if they are sufficiently discouraged, will rupture the therapeutic alliance. In Chapter 9 we will be considering in more detail the conscious and unconscious ways that clients may disempower the counsellor.

THE ROLE OF THE THERAPIST'S POWER AND RESPONSIBILITY WHEN WORKING WITH BOUNDARIES

As we saw with the example of David above, despite one of the central tenets of a successful counselling relationship being that of recognised equality between counsellor and client, the counsellor may well be perceived by the client as having an upper hand. We can probably identify many reasons for this, but it is of particular importance if the client is new to counselling and has not experienced the contracting of boundaries before. In this instance, the counsellor is seen as 'in charge', which can lead to the potential for an imbalance of understanding and expectations. We may have experienced this personally during our training when taking part in non-facilitated personal development or community groups and automatically looking to the lecturer for guidance.

Many clients may view the counsellor as an expert, especially if their previous experience of accessing help is from medical professionals, such as their General Practitioner (GP). In that relationship, the medical model of care pre-defines the doctor as an expert with the aim of interpreting symptoms, prescribing treatment and instilling professional confidence. However, counselling is based on a more social model of care that, in most modalities, views the client as the expert in their own life (and situation) whilst placing the counsellor as the expert in the use of advanced communication skills.

The therapeutic process is intended to increase the client's personal insight and coping skills. For the new client, it may have taken a long time and a lot of courage to book the first session, so we have a responsibility to be alert to signs of discomfort or nervousness. Most clients won't be at their most decisive and dynamic at this stage and it's more likely that they might feel vulnerable, lack confidence, be overly polite or caught up within their own world to the point of distraction. Having an experienced and confident guide to instigate a healthy, positive and equal relationship is, for many, a central element of the therapeutic process.

THE POTENTIAL IMBALANCE ON A NEW CLIENT

In this vein and, although not the case for all, the confusion and tur-moil that some clients are living with prior to entering counselling can mean they are out of practice maintaining clear boundaries to various areas of their life. The counsellor's role is very much to encourage the establishment of shared aspects of the relationship and to maintain a safety during the process. The structure that safe limits can provide, and managing the adherence to them, is designed to offer physical, emotional and psychological care. The responsibility of establishing and maintaining this care should be professional but warm and under-pinned by the guidance offered within our ethical framework. Such responsibility ensures that we instigate the discussion, negotiation and agreement of these boundaries but also ensures that our client contrib-utes at every level, being aware of the implications of all decisions agreed upon. To illustrate this, consider the previous example of Joe and his preferred length of session. Not agreeing how often to meet and how long for at the beginning of the first session would be confusing, unprofessional and unhelpful. An element of structure and stability is necessary to develop trust.

We have acknowledged that there is no hard and fast rule for con-tracting with new clients because the process will vary depending on interpersonal, intrapersonal and external factors. Clients referred to a hospital counselling service, self-referral to a private practice, or attending a local voluntary organisation, will be significantly different, but all require clarity, flexibility, transparency and negotiation. How we approach contracting with our client within the variety of these con-texts will be discussed further in the next chapter.

PRACTICAL ELEMENTS

In addition to this flexible and individualised approach, most counsel-ling services have document agreements in pro-forma paperwork that is routinely completed with every new client. This may include an assessment questionnaire or tool, a contract, possibly leaflets outlining the details of the service provision and client notes documentation that is maintained as a record of session content and progress. Although not a legal requirement, it is usually best practice to keep robust professional records on each client. In fact, if our practice is ever legally challenged, detailed but not excessive notes are a vital aid in documenting our work.

According to Bond and Mitchels, if there is an enquiry or inquest involving a client *'The lack of records may prevent the therapist from providing evidence ... Therefore it could make it much more likely that the therapist will have to give evidence in person'* (2008: 139). That being the case, the development and use of paperwork designed to meet the specific needs of your service can potentially reduce significant stress. Investing time on developing a pro-forma for use with clients attending the service is expected practice and allows you to incorporate a range of aspects that may be particular to your own service.

To illustrate this, it can be helpful to reflect on your current procedures. We have already considered some issues which might be viewed as challenging by some counsellors. Here are a selection of other situations. Read through each and consider how you might respond in each situation, then how you might approach documenting the process and outcome for your records.

- Caitlin has spent several sessions working through her anger. You make an observation but she vehemently disagrees with you.
- Alice consistently refers to her previous experience in counselling which was very different (better or worse).
- Colin has been working as a student counsellor within a college that only employs volunteer counsellors. They claim there is no budget to offer a salary.
- Kayleigh graduated from her diploma course and is working towards accreditation. She is constantly doubting her abilities and is convinced that her clients notice her lack of confidence.
- Kathleen has always had a poor memory and is worried that she will forget something a client said in a previous session.

Include suggestions for how to manage these challenges for each of the above scenarios.

- What might you do?
- How might you record this?

It might be helpful with formulating your approach to consider how Davies breaks the process down:

> Ethical decision making involves gathering facts, determining whether a problem or dilemma truly exists, and whether or not there is an ethical, legal, moral, professional or clinical issue involved. It uses a framework of client rights and professional obligations to make decisions. It is also the process of considering divergent courses of action and their implications and consequences for the client, as well as for the clinician or counsellor.

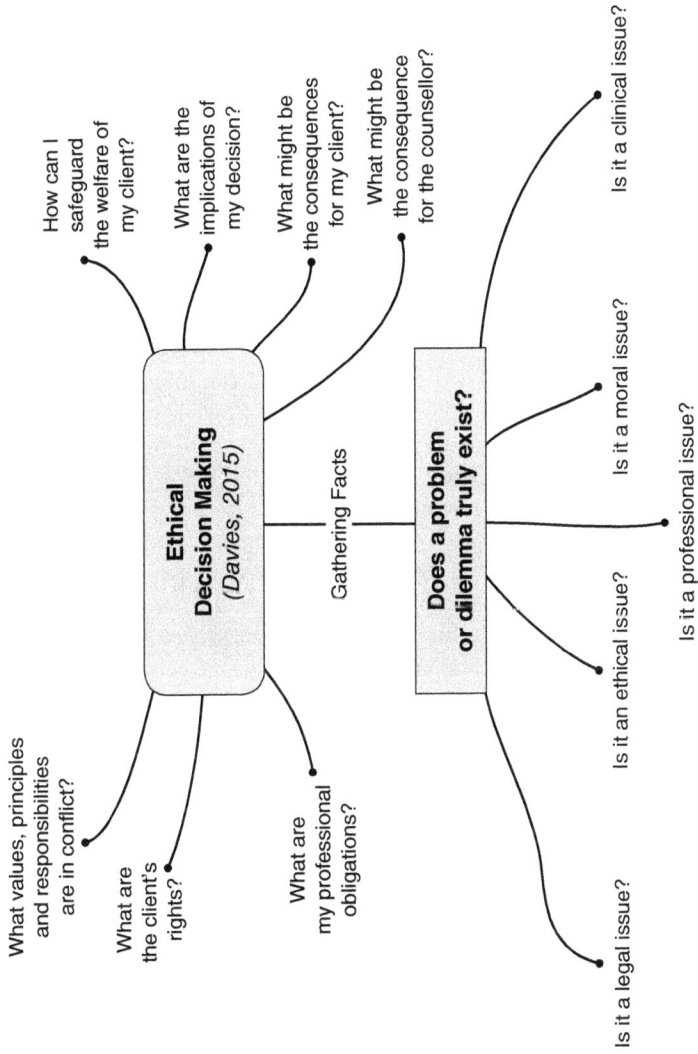

Ethical Decision Making
(Davies, 2015)

- How can I safeguard the welfare of my client?
- What are the implications of my decision?
- What might be the consequences for my client?
- What might be the consequence for the counsellor?
- What values, principles and responsibilities are in conflict?
- What are the client's rights?
- What are my professional obligations?

Gathering Facts

Does a problem or dilemma truly exist?

- Is it a clinical issue?
- Is it a moral issue?
- Is it a professional issue?
- Is it an ethical issue?
- Is it a legal issue?

Figure 2.4

It is making choices in the light of conflicting values, principles and responsibilities, and determining how best to safeguard the interests and welfare of clients. (Davies, 2015: 6)

By dissecting this we can end up with a flexible working framework that might look like Figure 2.4.

Extrapolating the definition like this allows us to create new perspectives, which we can use to help identify our choices and focus our decisions.

THE HISTORICAL CONTEXT TO THE DEVELOPMENT OF THINKING IN THIS AREA ACROSS THEORETICAL ORIENTATIONS

How boundaries are agreed and managed changes both over time and according to the cultural norms of the local community and wider society. Earlier in this chapter we touched on what we might consider to be Freud's flexible boundary management but at the time, these were considered acceptable. There weren't any ethical guidelines, examples of good practice or professional bodies to help. Issues relating to power imbalance were informed by the panacea of the time: the medical model of care with analysis being a new form of diagnosis. Early psychologists and talking therapists had to test to find what worked for their patients without the hindrance of external guidance. In much the same way, behavioural and cognitive theorists and practitioners also established their own methods of managing their working practice. Their focus was less on analysis (diagnosis) and more on treatment (prescription). The main difference was that their treatment was based on future actions, repetition, reframing and changing triggers in the environment as opposed to concentrating on understanding the past. This led to an increase in therapeutic sessions moving out of the therapy room and into the client's world. Ethical considerations and professional boundaries took on a wider role as flexibility grew.

By the 1940s, Humanistic therapists challenged what had gone before; they adopted a far more egalitarian approach placing the client in a different, more central role. The terms person-centred and client-centred were introduced by Carl Rogers to illustrate this shift. Patients became clients, the medical approach became more of a social approach and counsellors focused more on the uniqueness of the individual and the relationship. This brought with it a further development in ethical thinking which subsequently impacted on boundary setting.

Throughout the theoretical shifts that have driven the profession over the years, from Freud to the present day, the role of empirical evidence and relevant research have informed and underpinned practice. But historical development and research aren't the only influences on our boundary making.

CULTURAL DIFFERENCES AND SIMILARITIES

As well as historical differences, we should be aware that there are also significant cultural differences in regard to boundary setting which we should consider. Our cultural influences are influenced by the norms and values of the families, communities and societies that we were brought up in, as well as those we currently live in. They are formed by our traditions, expected and accepted behaviours, spiritual wellbeing and religious beliefs.

Where we are based geographically can have a significant impact upon what is recognised as acceptable therapeutic practice. It is easy to assume that due to the emphasis on psychological theory and scientific evidence behind therapeutic development that counselling is of a mainly secular nature. Admittedly, in the form we are referring to in this book, it is more commonly practised in the West. European, American and English-speaking countries, such as Australia, have a greater tradition of psychotherapeutic counselling whereas countries with a greater tradition of religious culture may understand 'counselling' as being of a different nature. For example, when working in Sri Lanka following the tsunami, local communities understood 'counselling' as giving advice and guidance. It was more common to visit a temple and request religious guidance from a monk than to reflect on personal emotions, reactions and coping strategies.

It may seem obvious to us what we mean by therapeutic counselling in our own practice but we can't assume that it is equally obvious to our clients. It is surprising how many new clients assume that counselling involves information and instruction. Explaining the process to every client within the contracting session is a key method of ensuring they can make an informed decision as to whether the methods we use are what they are expecting and fit in with their own world view.

There are numerous other ways in which we all make assumptions based on previous experiences. These might include family pressures, our gender, our sexuality, disability and religious practices such as expecting advice or guidance. Read these three situations and consider

(a) the cultural influences that have contributed to the situation
(b) how you might approach them within your therapy room
(c) where your values and world view lie in each scenario.

Example 1: Naseem told you that she is feeling pressured into an arranged marriage. She has agreed to the marriage as she is scared of how her family would react if she refused.

Example 2: Stefan was brought up in a very Catholic family. He explained to you that he has known that he has been gay since he was young but doesn't know how to tell his mother.

Example 3: Joan has just had a baby girl and is finding she can't bond with her. Joan and her husband are both deaf and she was devastated to discover that their daughter isn't.

Clearly there are no definite answers, but each example may have highlighted issues that show how your own experiences may be similar or different to those of our clients. This is why empathy is so crucial a skill, as it allows us to see the client's experience from their own perspective. At the same time the counsellor should be able to remain in their own world and not over-associate with that of their client; to recognise that the client's experiences are different from their own. Rogers explains it thus:

> To be with another in this way means that for the time being you lay aside the views and values you hold for yourself in order to enter another's world without prejudice. In some sense it means that you lay aside your self and this can only be done by a persona who is secure enough in himself that he knows he will not get lost in what may turn out to be the strange or bizarre world of the other, and can comfortably return to this world when he wishes. (Rogers, 1975: 2–10)

We can see from this that if we are skilful in the use of empathy, there is no need for us to have any previous experience of the client's world as it would be irrelevant. The use of empathy reinforces our ability, as counsellors, to work with any client from any background. The focus should rather be placed on our valuing of the individual client; their world view, upbringing and influences are then just seen as an integral part of the person themselves.

RELATIONSHIP BETWEEN BOUNDARY MANAGEMENT AND THE THERAPIST'S POWER AND RESPONSIBILITY

The aim with boundary setting is to achieve a balance that allows for safe and healthy change or development. This process is dependent upon the relationship that the counsellor and client build between them.

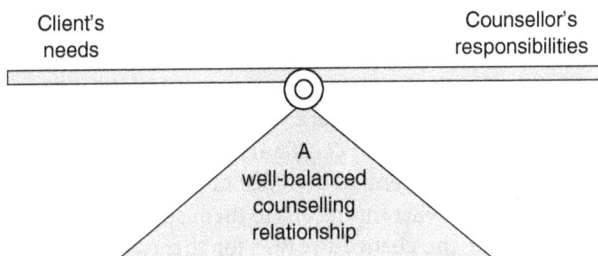

Figure 2.5

For healthy progress, there needs to be a sense of ownership by both parties rather than solely the counsellor. Even if they have previously engaged in counselling, a client attending for the first time often feels that they are at a disadvantage to the counsellor. Whilst the counsellor's experience and professional training informs their awareness of the context inside the therapy room, each counsellor is unique making each first meeting unpredictable. Meeting for a contracting session and an open discussion of boundaries to be agreed upon is a professional way to approach several issues:

- As all counsellors should do, discuss and agree boundaries; it's an immediate common ground that clients who have experience of counselling elsewhere will recognise.
- Discussing boundaries informs the client that there is flexibility in certain areas (such as timing, cost, venue, etc.).
- Discussing boundaries informs the client that there isn't flexibility in other areas but clarifies why (confidentiality, professional standards, law, etc.).
- Discussing boundaries affords the client a voice, an opportunity to share their intentions and hopes for the sessions.
- Discussing boundaries offers the chance to question each other and subsequently to make informed decisions.
- Discussing boundaries allows either party to decide that the relationship might or might not work before any investment is made.

- Discussing boundaries allows both parties to walk away. If the client decides the relationship might not be what they need, it is the counsellor's responsibility to offer the new client a choice of continuing or not.

These are all dependent on the setting. A statutory service will have policies, procedures and mandatory boundaries that differ from a voluntary or private service, and it is the counsellor's responsibility to explain them very clearly. Having literature, such as leaflets, that can be given to the client before or during that first session is very helpful in reducing the pressure on the client to memorise everything agreed.

Once the boundaries have been agreed, it is the counsellor's responsibility to manage them. How this is done is influenced by the theoretical orientation that we work within.

Let us imagine that a client constantly turns up 10 minutes late for their sessions. A person-centred therapist might point this out and ask the client to consider what this means to them and why they do it. The hope would be for the client to realise for themselves that this isn't helping them progress as quickly and to decide to address their time-keeping themselves. A psychodynamic counsellor may focus on any unconscious, as well as conscious, reasons for poor timekeeping in an effort to highlight any unhelpful defence mechanisms. A CBT therapist may concentrate more on the patterns of behaviour and what reward the client is gaining from the repetition which reinforces it.

Management of boundaries may not be comfortable for a new counsellor. Low confidence or fear of confrontation can generate powerful reservations. Maintaining the power balance means that we don't adopt a critical stance. It is not helpful or appropriate to reprimand or chastise our client. Raising awareness of the previous agreement to the boundary and an open discussion on the impact on the therapy are far more helpful. To touch on Eric Berne's (1961) explanation of ego states, we are not adopting the role of 'parent' counsellor to our 'child' client but rather aiming for an adult to adult dialogue to reinforce rather than diminish the relationship.

ETHICAL REQUIREMENTS

This whole process of maintaining balance has its foundation in ethical working. This is simply working with an awareness of what is right or wrong, safe or unsafe. However, such binary or dichotomised thinking is only one way of approaching decision making and this can cause much uncertainty, even with experienced counsellors.

As mentioned earlier, there is a balance to maintain between the tensions of law, working policies and our professional ethical frameworks. If we focus solely on the ethical frameworks this will help us interpret our legal and organisational responsibilities through professional filters. These guidelines are deliberately written in a general manner that allows interpretation for application by the practitioner. This is intentional to allow for the uniqueness of each situation. An assumption must be made that a practising counsellor should have the ability to weigh up a situation, consider all aspects and make a safe decision. If ethical guidelines are too prescriptive, they don't allow for necessary flexibility.

All counselling professional bodies publish ethical guidelines, which members are responsible for adhering to. They are explained to members in a manner that is underpinned by the ethos of the organisation. Some relevant examples are included here.

The Health Professions Council explain the standards of conduct, performance and ethics to registrants as such:

> If you make informed, reasonable and professional judgements about your practice, with the best interests of your service users as your prime concern, and you can justify your decisions if you are asked to, it is very unlikely that you will not meet our standards. By 'informed', we mean that you have enough information to make a decision. This would include reading these standards and taking account of any other relevant guidance or laws. By 'reasonable', we mean that you need to make sensible, practical decisions about your practice, taking account of all relevant information and the best interests of the people who use or are affected by your services. You should also be able to justify your decisions if you are asked to. (HPC, 2008: 5–6)

In Section 10.1, BABCP clearly instructs members regarding transparency and communication stating:

> You must explain to the service user the treatment you are planning on carrying out, the aims, rationale, risks involved and any alternative treatments. You must also explain if you see a service user only for evaluative or diagnostic procedures. If the treatment is experimental rather than established and proven, you must also explain this to the service user before consent is sought. You must make sure that you get their informed consent to any treatment you do carry out. You must make a record of the person's decisions for treatment and pass this on to other members of the health-care or social care team involved in their care. (BABCP, 2010: 11)

The issue of informed consent is crucial in almost every situation although there are some areas in law that require us to withhold informing the client of our actions. In section 1.3 of the BPS Standards of Informed Consent (BPS, 2009: 12) it is stated clearly that:

1. Ensure that clients, particularly children and vulnerable adults, are given ample opportunity to understand the nature, purpose, and anticipated consequences of any professional services or research participation, so that they may give informed consent to the extent that their capabilities allow.
2. Seek to obtain the informed consent of all clients to whom professional services or research participation are offered.
3. Keep adequate records of when, how and from whom consent was obtained.
4. Remain alert to the possibility that those people for whom professional services or research participation are contemplated may lack legal capacity for informed consent.

This can be compared with the guidance provided by UKCP (2009: 6, Section 7 of the Ethical Principles and Code of Ethical Contact) where it asserts

7.1 The psychotherapist undertakes to explain to the client, to the extent applicable to their modality and the client's capacity: the psychotherapist's clinical method(s) of working; and the client's choice to participate in any therapeutic interventions suggested by the psychotherapist including any commitments the psychotherapist makes to the client and any commitments the psychotherapist requires of the client.

7.2 The psychotherapist undertakes not to intentionally mislead a client concerning the type or nature of the psychotherapy practised.

7.3 The psychotherapist commits to clarify with clients the nature, purpose and conditions of any research in which the clients are to be involved and to ensure that informed and verifiable consent is given before commencement of the therapy and research.

These are just some examples to illustrate the differing levels of specificity provided by some of the major professional bodies counsellors join. These differ from standards of proficiency, which are also designed to protect the safety of clients by stipulating a level of safe working practice that is expected of members of that organisation. These, in combination with ethical frameworks, help counsellors with a structure to consider their contracting, boundaries and working with clients.

RESPONSIBILITIES OF THE THERAPIST

So far we have identified a range of situations that might require a level of professional reflection to ensure a balanced and ethically sound relationship. We have also pinpointed some relevant professional guidance, but what are our actual responsibilities within this? If we view each session with a client holistically, our responsibilities fall into several categories:

1. Safety for the client.
2. Safety for the counsellor.
3. Safety within the environment.
4. Development of the therapeutic process.

By working through each separately, our responsibilities can become more obvious. The following questions can help us focus on these areas:

- Has my client been actively involved in agreeing boundaries?
- Do I feel confident with my professional standards?
- Has the environment been risk assessed?
- How do both client and counsellor know if there has been any progress?
- Am I being transparent and honest with my client?
- How often do I meet my supervisor? Is this the minimum recommended or what I actually need?
- Do both client and counsellor feel it is private yet safe?
- How are we mapping progress?
- Is my client offered the opportunity to discuss their safety?
- Am I up to date with my legal responsibilities?
- Can other people overhear our session?
- Are both client and counsellor actively involved in the evaluation process?
- Is my client aware of the complaints procedure?
- Do I have a working knowledge of current policies and procedures?
- What would I do if at any time I didn't feel safe?
- What would I do if either of us felt stagnant?

There may be other, more relevant questions that can be added to this process depending upon the organisation providing the counselling service, or if in private practice. It is not sufficient to simply identify areas of difficult or potential issues, but we have a professional responsibility to actively engage with any challenges that become obvious, or we suspect might be present. Having a suspicion of unsafe practice comes hand in hand with action. For each of the above questions, we need to prepare a course of action so we are making changes to ensure safety for everyone involved. If we come across a situation in which we are unsure how to progress, Bond (2010) outlines a six-step framework to approach ethical problem solving which can be used to systematically work through a challenge. This is considered in Chapter 8.

AREAS FOR CONCERN AND POTENTIAL CHALLENGES

These are just some key areas to consider in relation to safety, but there are endless situations that may cause more general concern; it is well beyond the realm of this book to even attempt to identify them all. As a realistic alternative, here are five potential issues covering a range of areas that may present as a challenge to a counsellor. A short analysis of each will provide practice in demonstrating the process of facing up to situations that challenge our professional working practice.

1 Working with a very experienced client

New counsellors in particular may find it challenging or even off-putting to work with an experienced client. Concerns may be straightforward, such as feeling intimidated by their own lack of confidence or fear that their skills may be judged. However, there may be less obvious concerns.

> Bill was in the second year of his counselling diploma and on placement in an addiction service. His first client, Jeff had been attending the service sporadically for 12 years. During their contracting session Bill explained that he was a trainee and was disconcerted when Jeff told him 'not to worry' and 'I'll keep you right'. Bill took this to supervision and on further exploration felt that Jeff had a need to control or dominate the session and was unconsciously vying for dominance.

In this situation, Bill's supervisor was able to support and encourage him to examine his own response to this dynamic which allowed Bill to understand Jeff's perspective and to continue their relationship without feeling that he had been challenged or belittled.

2 Working with a passive client

Clients who have never had experience of being listened to or being heard may be resistant to being given a voice. Entering into an equal working relationship with a client who is used to being told what to do or bullied can be very challenging. It can take a considerable amount of time and persistence to instil empowerment and autonomy.

Sadie is attending counselling within a refuge following a 12-year abusive relationship. She presented as being very quiet. When asked about any previous experience with counselling she explained that there hadn't been an opportunity for her to get out of the house on her own for a while.

What would you consider to be your responsibility if Sadie was your client? How could you nurture an equal relationship?

3 Being client led

Any counselling relationship places the client at the centre of the session, regardless of orientation. This dynamic may be perceived as less professional by a new client expecting the counsellor to take control of a session, such as a GP might. Highlighting any flexibility in boundaries might surprise the client or reduce their confidence in a controlled or medical process.

Jasminda was referred by her family doctor. On first meeting, she states that she is expecting the counsellor to give her advice and point out what she can change to make her feel better. The counselling service based in the practice is person-centred and the counsellor works from the perspective that Jasminda is the expert in her own life.

If you were the counsellor in this situation, what would you see as being your responsibility? What might you do to support Jasminda in developing confidence in her own decision making?

4 Testing boundaries

Many people like to test boundaries, and clients are no different. In childhood this process is associated with developing independence, but adults also can follow similar patterns of behaviour. Examples that might present within the counselling room include wanting to extend a session by staying longer, forgetting to bring their session fee with them or asking if they can bring a friend in with them.

> During their first meeting at the contracting session the counsellor explained the session fee to Bernie and offered the choice of bank transfer or cash before the session began. Bernie explained that she had just changed banks and there was a problem with her setting up online banking. She paid for her first two sessions in cash. At the third session she explained that she had transferred the money electronically but on checking, the counsellor hadn't received it. This happened for three weeks in succession.

What is your responsibility in this situation and how might you address payment with Bernie in a manner that maintains the equality in the relationship? Would there be any consequences to your actions?

5 Manipulation

Despite many thinking that the counselling process can only be manipulated by an experienced client working with an inexperienced counsellor this is not the case. Any counsellor can, whether justifiably or not, feel they are being manipulated and this might or might not be the intention of the client.

> Frankie has been referred to your service by his social worker. You have met with him eight times and after every session he tells you that you are the only person that really understands him and that if he had more sessions, it would mean greater progress. He is only funded for ten sessions but he tells you that if he isn't referred for more there's no knowing what he might do to himself.

What might your assessment of this situation include? What would you discuss with Frankie and would you involve anyone else? What are your options?

Questions for reflection

- Use the Johari Window model to reflect upon your working with new and ongoing clients.
- What is your strategy for ensuring that you are working safely – both for yourself and your client?

When considering these questions, it might be helpful to introduce the following aspects:

1. Supervision.
2. Session notes.
3. Honesty and transparency with your client.
4. Keeping up to date regarding the law.
5. Referring to ethical guidelines and professional body.
6. Awareness and adherence to organisational policies and procedures.

Chapter summary

Hopefully you now have a grasp of the importance of our own ethical stance and how we recognise and manage power within the therapy room, along with the possible impact this can have upon our safety and that of our clients. Using a structure for reflecting on any ethical decisions is most helpful to see the bigger picture and reduce the risk of knee-jerk reactions. This is especially true if that structure:

- includes reflecting on our past experience (what worked and what didn't)
- considers our current practice and development
- takes a strategic stance in considering future situations we may not have experienced.

By being prepared we can increase our chances of having a confident response if they should occur.

FURTHER READING

Bond, T. (2010). *Standards and ethics for counselling in action* (3rd edn). London: Sage.

Icheku, V. (2011). *Understanding ethics and ethical decision making.* Bloomington, IN: Xlibris.

Thompson, M. (2010). *Understand ethics: teach yourself.* Oxon: Hodder Education.

Vardy, P., & Grouch, P. (1999). *The puzzle of ethics.* London: Fount.

SETTING OUT TOGETHER: CONTRACTING

Your success in building a safe alliance depends greatly upon your contract and the initial negotiation to clarify boundaries with clients. Embedded within this process there are therapeutic benefits but also occasional challenges when dealing with clients' expectations of counselling and the counsellor's role and relationship. This initial meeting should include reinforcing client autonomy and ensuring informed consent so that boundaries are clearly understood, whether they are agreed or imposed, whether they are face-to-face or via a digital platform. We need to reflect on our levels of transparency, making decisions regarding how we communicate this and understand how the pre-therapy contact reinforces our ethos. We need to also be evaluating our use of ongoing assessment measures and their efficacy for both our service and our clients. The contracting session is also an appropriate time to be assessing risk to embed safety within the contract and to identify how any risks to the therapeutic relationship might be avoided. To help with this, two examples of contracts are included in this chapter.

IMPORTANCE OF THE CONTRACT TO NEGOTIATE AND CLARIFY BOUNDARIES WITH CLIENTS

The glossary for the current BACP *Ethical Framework* (2016) defines contracting as

An agreement, written or oral, between the people involved about the terms on which goods or services will be provided. Any business and therapeutic terms and conditions that are agreed between counselling professionals and their clients will usually form part of the legal contract between them. Contracts are useful for reinforcing and clarifying practitioners' ethical commitments to their clients and can help to reduce uncertainty or disagreement, especially when recorded in writing. [GP32, 32a, 32b]

This clearly tells us that a counselling contract is a professional and legal requirement intended to improve clarity and safety and reduce dubiety.

There are many situations in everyday life where we contract our relationships, some formal, for example with a wifi provider, bank or educational establishment, and some informal, such as with friends and family. Contracts are necessary for the benefit of all parties involved as they clearly itemise the limits of the relationship being entered into; they are simply an agreement of how we will be working together. Until the 1960s counselling contracts consisted of the counsellor giving the client information about the service they provided, providing clerical details such as appointment time, cost and sometimes, an explanation of what might take place. It was then realised that empowering clients to take an active role in negotiating and clarifying a mutual contract could be very much part of the therapeutic process. Contracting is a method of demonstrating at the very onset of our relationship that we have the skill to communicate directly, avoid confusion and allow everyone involved to share aims, hopes and preferences. It might be a professional and legal requirement but it is simple to introduce in an accessible and supportive manner.

As previously mentioned, if we are to empower our client to take an equal role in the negotiation of the boundaries, we must ensure that we are aware of potential causes of inequality in therapy. We should be developing our confidence in challenging these causes to help our client become more involved and empowered to contribute to the contracting process. Equality and confidence increases the chances of our client's satisfaction with the agreement as it represents not simply the counsellor's expectations (and guiding rules) but theirs as well.

As an aside, it should also be mentioned here that contracting sessions are offered to allow clients an informed choice as to whether to book future sessions or not; there is much debate as to whether it is ethical to charge for this process. The arguments for charging are many but involve the counsellor's time, issues of value and professionalism and how the client views us. Arguments against charging for a first session concentrate more on the appropriateness to charge for a meeting where information is being swapped and questions are being asked. An equivalent might be asking a plumber for a detailed estimate for a planned extension. They would receive little business if they charged to provide an estimate. In reality there are ways round this such as charging a lower fee for the first session or charging the usual fee, which is then refunded if they book further sessions. Many counsellors integrate the contracting into the beginning of the first session so the hourly rate includes both contracting and the beginning of the therapeutic work. However, this might make it harder for new clients to leave half way through if they don't feel the service will meet their needs. For many counsellors, this decision is pre-set depending upon the setting they work in or the theoretical orientation that guides their work.

To summarise, contracting is a two-way process that ensures transparency of practice at the start of counselling and if we often return to it for evaluation during therapy, it will significantly reduce the chance for potential disputes in the future.

PRE-THERAPY CONTACT

Depending upon the setting you work within, it is likely that your first contact with a new client is prior to their first session. If you work in private practice or voluntary organisation they may telephone or email to request information or make an appointment. From the very first contact we have with our client, our manner and the content of that first communication can help or hinder the implementation of clear boundaries. We should consider carefully what is appropriate to discuss in a phone call and what to include in an email.

Ideally we should aim to provide information clearly and concisely stating exactly which aspects are negotiable and which are fixed. Our style should be friendly and approachable but still very professional and clear about details. The language should be appropriate to your client group so edit it for jargon and terminology. Some counsellors provide a short glossary at the end of any information to answer unasked questions. Ask your supervisor for their guidance and for a client's viewpoint ask a non-counselling colleague or friend to read it and feedback.

CLIENTS' EXPECTATIONS OF THERAPY AND THE THERAPIST

We can see these questions come from differing perspectives; the counsellor is mainly focusing on the client but the client is focusing on the service. Bearing this in mind and spending time on both, will have an immediate positive impact on the therapeutic relationship. Jack, a previous client demonstrates this clearly.

'I was really embarrassed about attending and had put off booking a first session for ages. When I arrived I didn't have a clue about what would happen. My best friend's wife had suggested I try counselling but she had never been either so wasn't any help. Making the appointment was really difficult for me and I was so uncomfortable that I forgot all my questions. I just hoped the counsellor would keep me right.'

Jack was motivated by his desire for change. When asked why he made the appointment he said '*I just got sick of avoiding dealing with my situation and being really unhappy.*' We can see from this example that the power balance was clearly skewed in favour of the counsellor. Jack acknowledged that he had been expecting to be quite passive in the process. The counsellor however, expected Jack to take an active involvement in the initial meeting and intended for them to contribute equally. By ensuring that all questions were clear and justified, the counsellor encouraged Jack to take an active role.

Although in this case Jack had few pre-formed expectations, there are a range of influences that can shape the client's expectations. To understand our client holistically, it is relevant to consider not just their previous experiences but also other aspects of their lives that can shape who they are. The list here is in no way finite but might include any family pressures, their gender, sexuality, any seen or unseen disability, their faith and religious practices and the environment they are living in. Every one of these aspects shapes who our client is today and helps us to approach contracting in a way that deepens the connection with them. It is also a time when we begin to understand what makes them who they are which in turn contributes to the therapeutic alliance.

Such information can be gathered very easily by including questions in a pre-intake questionnaire, assessment form or booking page on a website. The client only provides the information they are happy with you knowing and it allows for the service to be moulded specifically to each and every client. This is in no way an interrogation but by taking a relaxed and interested approach to unseen and unknown aspects and avoiding being inquisitive contributes to the client-focus by placing them firmly at the centre of the session.

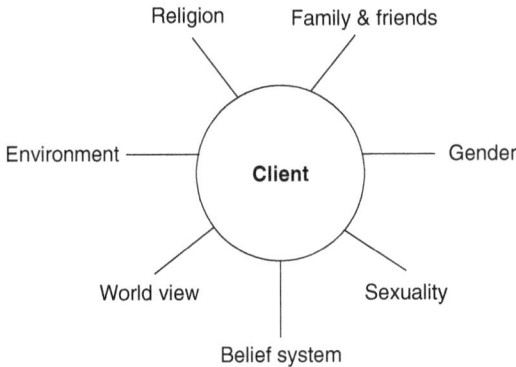

Figure 3.1

MAKING DECISIONS REGARDING DEPTH OF TRANSPARENCY

How much we share with our client is not pre-determined. Insufficient information can leave a client feeling unsure or confused whereas offering too much information can be unhelpful and overwhelming. The BACP has provided some very straightforward advice regarding this. The table below is included in the BACP resource document *Good Practice in Action 039: Commonly Asked Questions Resource: Making the Contract within the Counselling Professions* by Heather Dale (2016).

Table 3.1 *Ethical framework for the counselling professions principles (Dale, 2016)*

Personal Moral Qualities (PMQs)	
Care: 'benevolent, responsible and competent attentiveness to someone's needs, wellbeing and personal agency'	What strategies do I have in place to make sure that the client completely understands the contract?
Diligence: 'the conscious deployment of skills and knowledge needed to achieve a beneficial outcome'	Am I clear about the limits of my competence?
Courage: 'the courage to act in spite of known fears, risks and uncertainty'	Will I be able to ask for payment for missed sessions even when I am anxious that it might alienate the client?

(Continued)

Table 3.1 *(Continued)*

Personal Moral Qualities (PMQs)	
Empathy: 'the ability to communicate understanding of another person's experience from that person's perspective'	Is my contract written in language that is easily understood?
Humility: 'the ability to assess accurately and acknowledge one's own strengths and weaknesses'	Have I asked a trusted professional to read my contract and feed back any perceived issues?
Identity: 'sense of self in relationship to others that forms the basis of responsibility, resilience and motivation'	Does my contract give a clear sense of who I am and what the boundaries of this relationship will be?
Integrity: 'commitment to being moral in dealings with others, including personal straightforwardness, honesty and coherence'	Is my contract fair?
Resilience: 'the capacity to work with the client's concerns without being personally diminished'	What have I said about out of session contact? Have I been clear about my limits?
Respect: 'showing appropriate esteem for people and their understanding of themselves'	Is my contract written in clear and respectful language?
Sincerity: 'a personal commitment to consistency between what is professed and what is done.'	Do I believe in what I have said?
Wisdom: 'possession of sound judgement that informs practice'	Has my client agreed these terms verbally and in writing?

Working through this list with the accompanying questions can be a reaffirming process, especially if you have used the same contracting paperwork, structure or explanations for some time. This can be worked through with your supervisor who might be able to add an alternative perspective or challenge some of your assumptions or blind spots.

HOW ATTENDING TO THE PROCESS OF CONTRACTING CAN BE PROFOUNDLY USEFUL THERAPEUTICALLY

On a very basic level, the activity of sitting quietly and patiently with a client, allowing them the space to explain why they are looking to attend therapy may be an everyday activity for us. However, the potential impact upon our client of being involved can be very powerful. To illustrate this, here is an example of how the contracting process can impact on our client in a positive way.

Rachael lived at home caring for her elderly parents for all her adult life until her father died last year and her mother died six months ago. She has approached your private practice as she is feeling lost and alone and says that she *doesn't know what to do with herself*. You invite her to attend a contracting session to give her the opportunity to meet with you, ask questions and find out if your service is the right one for her. You realise very quickly that her life until recently has been focused on helping others, as she is quiet, subdued and appears uncomfortable when answering questions about herself. When you ask for her opinion about how often she would like to meet, she answers 'I don't know, what do you think best?'. When you ask her what she would like to gain from attending sessions she states that she's not sure.

How could you help empower Rachael so she can identify her own goals? In what ways might the contracting process be beneficial to Rachael?

To help empower her, you might have considered not simply offering options but explaining the implications of each so Rachael is encouraged to make her own decisions. An open discussion regarding confidentiality early in the meeting might put her mind at rest regarding privacy and allow her the freedom to decide on whether she can trust you or not. By demonstrating through your skills that you aren't there to criticise or belittle her in any way, may be reassuring.

The contracting process may help Rachael understand that she can control aspects of her life. Rather than deferring to others, she is in a position whereby she can identify and explain her own needs. The discussion, options and contextualising within the negotiation process is enabling Rachael to make and test decisions in a safe environment with no unpleasant consequences. As her counsellor, you can balance the power within the relationship by providing sufficient information for Rachael to make informed choices based on her own needs, a situation she hasn't often found herself in.

CLIENT AUTONOMY AND INFORMED CONSENT

Whilst learning about our new client in this first session, we have a professional and legal responsibility to demonstrate safe practice. Two of the central ethical considerations of contracting are those of client autonomy and establishing informed consent. Client autonomy, the freedom for self-direction within safe limits underpins many models of therapy as it is based on a person-centred ethos. An autonomous client is free to take control and direct the content of the session according to their current needs. In this situation, the counsellor follows the client's lead whilst ensuring that the previously agreed boundaries are maintained. The level of autonomy permitted when originally agreeing those boundaries is not limited but depends upon the setting and therapeutic orientation of the counselling.

The second issue is that of informed consent. For our client to be sufficiently empowered to make informed decisions in relation to aspects such as their health, future and safety, we have a responsibility to ensure that they are aware of contributing factors and possible consequences. If counselling within the UK it is important to be aware that there are slight differences between the laws of the four nations regarding informed consent, especially with respect to working with children and young people. In England and Wales, Gillick competency is case law whereby a young person under 16 years of age is not automatically deemed legally competent but can be if they can demonstrate '*sufficient understanding and maturity to enable them to understand fully what is proposed*'. If your potential young client insists that their family should not be informed of their attending counselling, you should respect their confidentiality unless it puts them at risk of serious harm. The law in Northern Ireland is similar to that of England and Wales

In Scotland, the Age of Legal Capacity (Scotland) Act (1991) (S2(4)) states that a competent person under 16 years of age can consent to medical treatment if they can demonstrate that they are able to understand what is involved and any possible consequences. The National Guidance for Child Protection in Scotland (Scottish Government, 2014) states: '*In general, information will normally only be shared with the consent of the child (depending on age and maturity). However where there is a risk to a child's wellbeing, consent should not be sought and relevant information should be shared with other individuals or agencies as appropriate*'. How we approach informing clients to ensure consent has its foundation in the ethical guidelines of the professional organisation we are governed by. To illustrate this, the examples below are taken

Table 3.2 Applying BACP Ethical Framework for the Counselling Professions

	Commitment to clients	How I achieve this within my own practice
1. Put clients first by:	a. making clients our primary concern while we are working with them.	
2. Work to professional standards by:	a. working within our competence.	
	b. keeping our skills and knowledge up to date.	
	c. collaborating with colleagues to improve the quality of what is being offered to clients.	
	d. ensuring that our wellbeing is sufficient to sustain the quality of the work.	
	e. keeping accurate and appropriate records.	
3. Show respect by:	a. valuing each client as a unique person.	
	b. protecting client confidentiality and privacy.	
	c. agreeing with clients on how we will work together.	
	d. working in partnership with clients.	
4. Build an appropriate relationship with clients by:	a. communicating clearly what clients have a right to expect from us.	
	b. communicating any benefits, costs and commitments that clients may reasonably expect.	
	c. respecting the boundaries between our work with clients and what lies outside that work.	
	d. not exploiting or abusing clients.	
	e. listening out for how clients experience our working together.	
5. Maintain integrity by:	a. being honest about the work.	
	b. communicating qualifications, experience and working methods accurately.	
	c. working ethically and with careful consiceration of the law.	
6. Demonstrate accountability and candour by:	a. being willing to discuss with clients any known risks involved in the work and how best to work towards our client's desired outcomes.	
	b. ensuring that clients are promptly informed about anything important that has gone wrong in our work together, whether clients are aware of it, and quickly taking action to limit or repair any harm as far as possible.	
	c. reviewing our work with clients in supervision.	
	d. monitoring how clients experience our work together and the effects of our work with them.	

from the *BACP Ethical Framework for the Counselling Professions* where our commitment to clients is very clearly specified.

Complete the column on the right in Table 3.2 to demonstrate how you offer a safe service that addresses the needs of clients whilst ensuring that their agreement to attend is based on a clear understanding of the process.

The connections between informed consent and ethical implications are strong. As practitioners working with potentially vulnerable people, we have a duty of care to monitor and manage safety. We can see from the list of how we are to commit to our clients that it is our responsibility to ensure that we are totally honest and unambiguous when explaining not just the boundaries stipulated within the contract but also the therapeutic process, any potential consequences of counselling and our professional limits.

IMPACT OF HOW BOUNDARIES ARE AGREED

The method with which we agree or, perhaps, impose aspects of the contract will have an impact upon our relationship and on future interaction. It may seem obvious but if we are seen by our client to be clear, knowledgeable, confident and approach the process from a position of care, they will experience us very differently to a counsellor who is unsure, unclear, forgetful or unhelpful. Which category we fall into can be influenced by the amount of relevant information we provide including any literature we make available. The more detail the client can access prior to entering the counselling service, the greater the opportunity for them to make an informed decision about engaging with our service. Unambiguous materials that highlight the transparency of the process can set the scene for discussions on the foundations underpinning the process. Clients can access formal information on us and our service from a range of sources such as leaflets, website and adverts but can include informal sources such as reputation and word of mouth. Any aspects of our service that are flexible (such as cost, timing, etc.) and inflexible (confidentiality, venue) should be clearly stated.

FORMULATING A CONTRACT

The following are aspects commonly included in counselling contracts and can be used to assist you in formulating your own framework. It is recommended that each aspect discussed and agreed upon is documented and a copy given or made available to the client. If you have been working with the same organisational contract for some time, it may be beneficial to use this list to revisit and re-evaluate its effectiveness. Most contracts cover a range of business, therapeutic and logistical information.

Assessment

Our methods of assessment and case formulation. This may include any tools that we use, how regularly we evaluate progress and should also include risk.

Beginnings and endings

The process of therapy should be outlined to alleviate potential worries, as well as dependency or avoidance issues. Sharing information regarding the intended process also reduces any potential power imbalance. New clients may not be aware of the potential to feel worse before they feel better and that this may be a key part of their progress.

Competence

We have an ethical responsibility to inform our client of our professional status. It should be explained if you have membership of a professional association or are a trainee on placement. This tells our client of our experience and any professional connections.

Confidentiality

What limits there are to your service and your policy and procedures should also be explained to your client to ensure they are aware and happy with your professional and legal limits. Knowledge of current law and organisational policy is crucial.

Contracts

The contact itself should be discussed to clarify your working agreement highlighting its purpose and that, as a working document, aspects can be revisited and renegotiated throughout the time working together.

Complaints procedure

It is an ethical requirement that internal and external complaints procedures are clearly explained. Internal complaints refer to a line manager within the counselling service and external complaints would involve the professional body that the counsellor is a member of.

Dual relationships

This is discussed in more depth in Chapter 5, but can be summarised as what you might do if you were to encounter your client in a different environment and the reasons for that.

Missing/rescheduling a session

Is there a cost implication if the client does not turn up for their session? Does this differ from if they give more or less than 24 hours' notice or if they give no notice? The manner in which we manage attendance can have a significant impact upon reducing absence rates and differs between settings.

Monitoring and evaluation through reflective practice

How do we identify and monitor progress, successes and areas for further development? Whether this process is ongoing or carried out at intervals and how this is accomplished should be explained clearly. Clients may wish to see any evaluation tools before using them.

Number of sessions

How many times you meet can be determined by the setting (and therefore available funding). Asking the client what they intend, explaining your usual practice and including reference to the importance of evaluation and flexibility ensures that the client is completely aware of the agreement.

Record keeping

Clients can wonder what is documented following a session and who has access to the information. This can include a signed copy of the contract, session notes, any completed evaluation tools and copies of safe plans and any other relevant paperwork. The records we keep, their range and depth is very much dependent upon the service we work within.

Referral

Referring a client to another service may be inevitable but any methods and reasons should be fully explained. This is to ensure the client understands that they are being guided toward a more suitable service and doesn't interpret the process as rejection or that their issue is too difficult to be managed by the current counsellor. If assessment is carried out as a discrete process prior to a client starting counselling, it might not include the counsellor at all.

Roles

Aspects such as the function of the counsellor and required participation by the client will clarify what each will be contributing to the process. It is surprising the number of clients who are unaware of the level of depth into internal processes that counselling can involve. We should never assume a client's understanding of levels of processes.

Settings

The organisation, service or practice offering counselling has a strong influence on the design, contents and dissemination of the contract as well as each individual aspect. It may be important for a client to be aware of organisational policy in certain areas. Working alone in private practice comes with the responsibility of ensuring all boundaries are appropriately agreed and recorded according to the policies written by the counsellor.

Storing notes

If notes are being taken (and it is not a legal requirement to do so) their storage must be in line with current data protection legislation. We are required to review how long we store notes for and be able to justify why the length of time is appropriate. We should consider what we record, and why we hold the information we do. We must assess if information we keep is relevant, how we update it, store it and delete any out of date information. Finally, we should consider the security of the method in which we destroy or delete notes.

Supervision

The fact that you are engaged in an additional professional relationship that involves the client is relevant. Explain the type of supervision you receive (monitoring, educational, supportive, etc.) and the confidentiality surrounding that process.

Theoretical orientation

Clients have a right to know the underpinning modality we work within. Gaining even a rudimentary understanding of our theoretical ethos or assumptions will allow the client a deeper understanding of motivating factors to the way we work.

Timing of sessions

The setting and your working hours can determine when you meet. Appointments may be allocated by an external agency or be arranged at the end of the previous session. They may be flexible or pre-booked for the same time each week. Explaining the process and any opportunity for negotiation to the client will hopefully reduce missed appointments.

Training and experience

The qualifications, experience and professional development of the counsellor might not always be overtly discussed during the first meeting but should be available and easily accessible for a client to see. Depending upon the modality being used, this information might be included in the service's literature and any online presence, whereby in the past framed certificates in the waiting room were more of the norm.

EXAMPLE OF CONTRACT

Here are two examples of counselling contracts; one for a service within an organisation and the other in private practice. Although there are similarities, each is aimed at a different client base so is worded slightly differently to be appropriate. You are welcome to adapt these to meet the needs of your service.

Contract for Organisational Counselling Service

This contract is between

_____ (client) and _____ (counsellor)

Booking system

You can book a counselling session in two ways; either on the student intranet or via the college app. Log onto the intranet, click on the 'counselling' tab and choose your preferred campus from the dropdown menu. You will then see available appointments for the following week. Click on the session you would like. It is important that you do not arrange sessions for during a timetabled class. An email confirming the date and venue for your session and the name with email address of your counsellor will automatically be sent to your academic email address. Attached to this email is a pre-intake assessment form which we ask that you complete prior to your first session and email it to your counsellor.

What will happen?

The service is provided to help you identify and overcome any barriers that are preventing you succeeding in your studies. Your counselling sessions will last for 50 minutes. An important element of our service is that you will not be told what to do or given solutions. Instead, your counsellor recognises that you know your situation better than they do and they will help you to reflect and identify any ways in which you can alter something to feel happier. There is no charge for sessions as they are funded by the college.

Confidentiality and records

The content of the sessions is confidential, although your counsellor may need to discuss their work with their clinical supervisor. This is anonymous and is about maintaining their professional standards and will not pass on identifiable information about you. Your attendance code (not your name) may occasionally be included in an internal email, between counsellor and service manager for example. This will only be done in the event of administrative organisation or regarding a query and not include any other identifiable information. On very rare occasions if they discover there is a need to communicate with other professionals, this will only proceed after first letting you know what is to be shared and why. Brief records will be kept after each session but are stored securely. You are free to request access to these at any time

(Continued)

(Continued)

although you are not identified in them. We will always recommend that you inform your GP that you are attending our service.

Your attendance to the counselling service is not passed on to any other department in the college.

Cancellation

We do not have counsellors based in the college so they will be coming in for your appointment. Please aim to arrive 5 minutes early. In any event of your counsellor not being able to attend your session they will give you as much notice as possible by your chosen method of contact and offer you an alternative time. If you are unable to attend, please contact your counsellor (by email or phone) with at least 24 hours' notice. If you miss a session without contacting your counsellor, you will receive an email from your counsellor checking that you are OK and you will automatically be booked a session for the following week. However, if you miss a second session without notice, your counsellor will assume that this isn't the right time for you and you will need to re-book via the booking system, if there are any available appointments. Please note that this is likely to be with a different counsellor.

Our relationship

Your counsellor will remain discreet at all times. If you accidentally meet outside the sessions, they will acknowledge you in a brief and friendly manner unless you would rather that they didn't. It is not appropriate to discuss any issues with them unless it is within an arranged session.

Ending

You will initially be offered six sessions but this will be evaluated and reviewed as you progress. There may be a time in counselling when you feel upset or that counselling isn't helping. Please discuss this with your counsellor rather than stopping attending so you can consider the situation together. Usually, you will know when you are ready to end counselling and together we will find the way that feels comfortable for you to do this.

Referral

Although we are a college service, we do have links with local external agencies. If you feel you would benefit from additional support, or would like to be referred to another agency, please ask your counsellor. They will be happy to support your request to attend elsewhere. Equally, if your counsellor feels that a different organisation may be able to provide more specialised help than they can, they will give you relevant information.

Complaints

If there are any aspects of the counselling service that you are unhappy with, please discuss this with your counsellor in the first instance. If you feel your concern has not been fully addressed, please contact the service manager by email. The address can be found on the student intranet or the college app. They will do all they can to help. If you are still dissatisfied, your issue will be forwarded to the Director of Student Services and be processed in line with the college complaints procedure, again available on the student intranet.

Please read this document carefully and check it is what we have agreed together today. Unless you have any queries, these are our boundaries and ground rules that will enable us to work together. If you wish to discuss or negotiate any changes, I will be happy to chat about this before we sign.

This agreement is fully understood and agreed to and is signed as it stands by:

Private Practice Counselling Contract

This contract is between
_____ (client) and _____ (counsellor)

Booking system

Please telephone or email to make an appointment. My contact details are on the front of this leaflet. My working hours are Monday – Thursday 6.30pm – 8.30pm. I offer either face to face meetings or VOIP sessions (e.g. Skype).

What will happen?

Counselling sessions will usually last for 50 minutes. An important element of our service is that you will not be told what to do or given solutions. Instead, I provide the time and space for you to reflect and will support you to identify ways in which you would like to change or develop.

(Continued)

(Continued)

Cost

One 50-minute session costs £45.

Six 50-minute sessions cost £240

This is payable in advance by bank transfer or cheque.

Cancellation

If you wish to cancel a session, this can be done by text or email. I will reply within 24 hours.

Sessions cancelled with seven or more days' notice will be rescheduled without charge.

Sessions cancelled with less than seven days' notice will be charged at £20.

Sessions cancelled with less than 24 hours' notice will be charged at full rate.

Confidentiality and records

The content of sessions is confidential although I will discuss my work with my clinical supervisor. On rare occasions (involving legal responsibilities and/or risk) I may need to communicate with other professionals but this will only proceed after first letting you know what is to be shared and why. Brief records will be kept after each session but are stored securely. You are free to request access to these at any time. I would request that you do not identify me on social media.

Our relationship

If we meet accidentally outside the sessions, I will not acknowledge you unless you greet me first. This is simply so that if you are with anyone you don't have to explain who I am. It is not appropriate to discuss any issues unless within a pre-arranged session.

Ending

You can book as many sessions as you feel you need but this will be evaluated and reviewed as you progress. There may be time in counselling when you feel upset or that counselling isn't helping. Please let me know rather than stopping attending so we can consider the situation together. Usually, you will know when you are ready to cease counselling and together we will find the way that feels comfortable for you to do this.

Referral

If you feel you would benefit from additional support or would like to be referred elsewhere, please ask as I am happy to support your request to attend elsewhere. Equally, if I feel that a different organisation may be able to provide more specialised help than I can, I will give you relevant information.

Complaints

If there are any aspects of the counselling service that you are unhappy with, please discuss this with me in the first instance. If you feel your concern has not been fully addressed, I am a member of the BACP and as such abide by their professional standards. You are able to report any complaints directly to them via the contact details on the back of this leaflet.

Please read this document carefully and check it is what we have agreed together today. Unless you have any queries, these are our agreed boundaries that will enable us to work together. If you wish to discuss or negotiate any changes, I will be happy to discuss this before we sign.

This agreement is fully understood and agreed to and is signed as it stands by:

CHALLENGES OF DEALING CLEARLY WITH THE CONTRACTING PROCESS

Due to the nature of counselling, whichever sector you work in, you will enter into a range of professional interactions and encounter a diverse selection of people. Because of this, the amount of information provided within the contracting session may vary from client to client, depending upon their previous experiences in therapy. When starting out in counselling training it can be challenging to know the balance of how much detail is sufficient. It is common to feel embarrassment when discussing money, to have a lack of confidence in our own knowledge of current legal requirements or ethical guidelines or a discomfort with introducing these aspects directly. Any of these discomforts can lead us to fall into the trap of concentrating solely on our own expectations with regard to the management of a counselling process. This may feel like safe ground but taking the risk to allow the client to share their preferences and to explain their reasons is the first natural step of the therapeutic process.

Considering the client's expectations and ensuring that they are discussed and taken into consideration makes for a significantly fairer and more professional working relationship. Asking a client relevant questions to provide context during our first meeting can prevent the build up of anxiety and help us to make sure that we are both working with similar aims. Using empathy during this initial process can help us alter our own perspective and assumptions to understand the client's viewpoint. It can also help us identify areas for professional development. These are some examples to illustrate the differences:

Counsellors' questions tend to focus on the client themselves:

- Have you attended counselling before?
- Why have you chosen to come to counselling?
- What do you hope will take place when we meet?
- What would you like to be the outcome?
- How comfortable are you with talking about thoughts and feelings?

Clients' questions are more likely to relate to the sessions:

- How often should we meet?
- What are we going to do together?
- What will you expect me to do?
- How much will sessions cost?
- How many sessions should I attend?
- Where will we meet?
- Do you tell anyone what we talk about?
- Do you take notes and if so, can I see them?
- How qualified/experienced/good are you?

ASSESSING RISK

As contracting is designed to establish a safe and agreed working environment, there is a necessity to be aware of the wider context of the client's world. For us to work together therapeutically, our client needs to feel secure both in the relationship but also when they leave the counselling room. In relation to this, consider the following three questions:

1. What do you consider to be 'risk'?
2. What situations have your clients disclosed that you would consider to involve risk?
3. How are you at risk?

The Oxford English Dictionary (ODE, 2010: 1534) defines risk as '*a situation involving exposure to danger*', '*the possibility that something unpleasant or unwelcome will happen*' and '*person or thing regarded as a threat or likely source of danger*'. This allows for a broad understanding that incorporates a range of situations that clients may share with us. We should have strategies in place for assessing, monitoring and supporting our client in managing and reducing their risk. By being prepared, we can respond in a manner that is calm yet professional. This may come naturally from experience although developing the habit of working through potential scenarios can help prepare for a range of eventualities. Bear in mind that how we assess risk may be very different to how our client does. Because of this, we should plan how we might respond if we find ourselves working with a client who we feel is at risk but they disagree. Alternatively, we might be working with a client who feels at risk when we aren't clear about why or how.

The evaluation and assessment of risk should be approached both holistically and collaboratively. Figure 3.2 identifies a range of aspects that can be used to provide a workable structure. It highlights some of the key areas that might be considered to involve risk. When assessing risk, consider the client's world holistically and their sense of threat. As with most situations it is easier to view from different perspectives. Breaking the situation down into different areas can bring clarity and make it easier to work together with the client to consider each.

This exercise is designed to raise our awareness of how we perceive and interpret risk. Rearrange the following in order of risk and ask a counselling colleague or your supervisor to do the same. Then compare lists to highlight how we can all assess risk differently. You'll notice they are slightly vague which is intentional.

1. Being bullied by a colleague.
2. Living with a violent partner.
3. Engaging in unsafe sex.
4. Driving without wearing a seatbelt.
5. Maintaining three jobs.
6. Riding a motorbike.
7. Drinking alcohol every night.
8. Taking ecstasy in night clubs.

There is no right or wrong answer but complete the reordering process again with the list below which has a little more detail.

1. Being bullied by a colleague – and considering suicide because of it.
2. Living with a violent partner – and planning how to hurt them back.

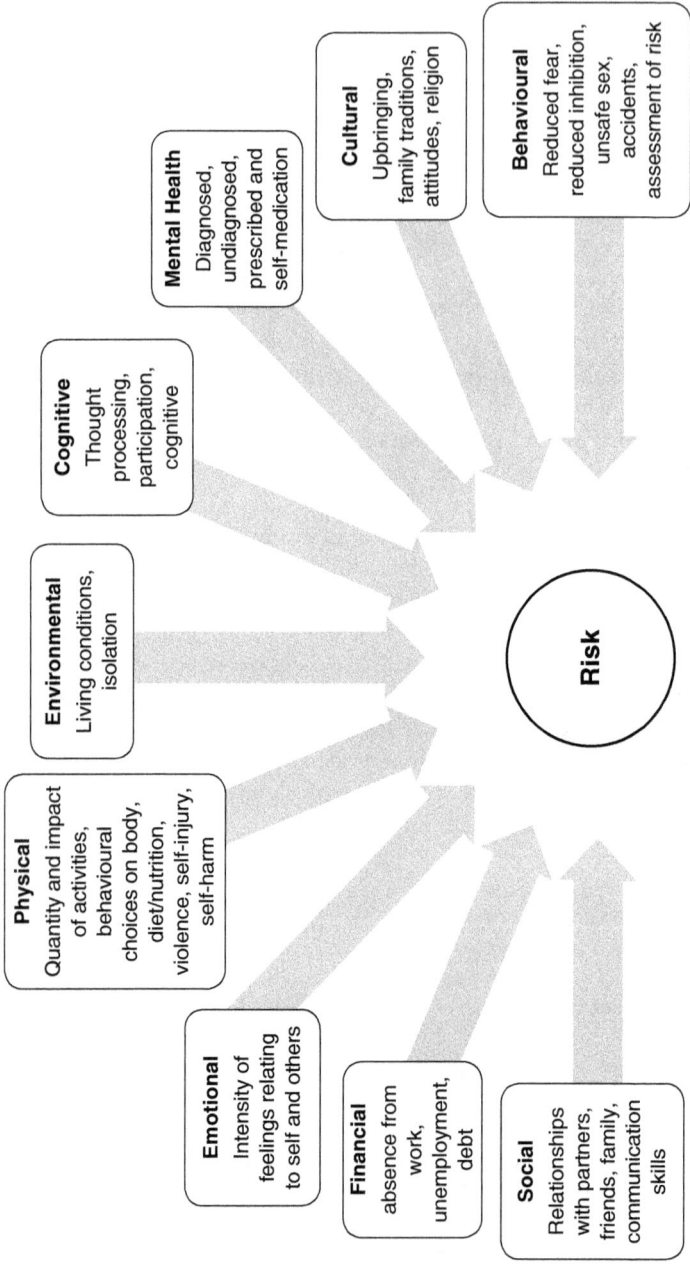

Physical
Quantity and impact of activities, behavioural choices on body, diet/nutrition, violence, self-injury, self-harm

Environmental
Living conditions, isolation

Cognitive
Thought processing, participation, cognitive

Mental Health
Diagnosed, undiagnosed, prescribed and self-medication

Cultural
Upbringing, family traditions, attitudes, religion

Behavioural
Reduced fear, reduced inhibition, unsafe sex, accidents, assessment of risk

Emotional
Intensity of feelings relating to self and others

Financial
absence from work, unemployment, debt

Social
Relationships with partners, friends, family, communication skills

Risk

Figure 3.2

3. Engaging in unsafe sex – with an ex-partner.
4. Driving without wearing a seatbelt – on the way home from the pub.
5. Maintaining three jobs – one of which is night shift.
6. Riding a motorbike – in street racing competitions.
7. Drinking alcohol every night – 125ml red wine.
8. Taking ecstasy in night clubs – once a year.

Again, there is no right or wrong answer but the additional detail may have changed the order of your answers. The purpose of this is to help explore our assumptions and see that additional information may change the way we view a situation. Of course our client will have significantly more information, which will give us a more accurate picture of any risk.

If we do feel our client is at risk, we have decisions to make about our next steps. Some decisions are pre-determined by the law or our organisational procedures, but those that aren't require examination, ethical decision making and open and honest discussion with both our client and supervisor. Following assessment, you should have agreed plans in place if the danger is imminent, if it is chronic or if it is potential. Agreeing a safe plan for imminent risk can be reassuring for a client as they have a tangible plan with them to take home. This is a simple list of options that they can take if they experience a crisis between sessions. This is an example but they should be designed around the client's needs and identified support:

Start at the first step, and should a person at any step be unavailable, move onto the next step.

1. Contact your GP on ....
2. Contact a named family member/friend/neighbour and ask them to watch over you. This should be someone you feel comfortable disclosing that you feel suicidal/are struggling with suicidal thoughts, so that they know why you are asking them to watch over you

   Person 1   ....
   Person 2   ....

3. Contact Breathing Space on 0800 83 85 87, or Samaritans on 08457 90 90 90
4. Contact NHS 24 on 111
5. Report to A&E

A safe plan is very different to a no-harm or no-suicide contract which is considered unethical by many counsellors. This is where a client is asked to sign a contract agreeing to not harm themselves for the duration of attending counselling, subsequently taking control and power out of their hands. It is argued to be non-client-centred for this reason, but is used widely in some medical settings as part of other support methods.

We should bear in mind that risk within the therapy room isn't one-sided. As counsellors, we must also reflect on our own risk taking to evaluate our self-care, some of which might not be obvious. The list below includes a small selection of professional risk that we might be working with:

- Out of date practice.
- Awareness of law, policies, procedures.
- Written recording of sessions.
- Not adhering to agreed boundaries.
- Overwork.
- Not saying 'no'.
- Poor planning – client work and supervision.
- Risky behaviours.
- Issues of transference.
- Dependency.

Consider each point on the list above identifying your strengths, weaknesses and any strategies you have in place for monitoring and managing the risk in your practice. Then reflect on the following questions in relation to your own practice.

- How might risk impact on your contracting?
- How might risk impact on your empathic understanding?
- How might risk impact on your trust?
- How might risk impact on your supervision?
- How might risk impact on your use of skills, e.g. challenge?

This may bring up areas to discuss in supervision. For a deeper exploration of these issues, this subject is covered in more detail in the text *Working with Risk in Counselling and Psychotherapy* by Andrew Reeves, also in the Essential Issues series.

Questions for reflection

Consider your current method for assessing risk then reflect on the following questions.

1. What is your current practice?
2. What do you consider to be the most successful aspects of this process?
3. Have you identified any areas of concern?
4. How can your risk assessment process be improved?
5. When is risk healthy and therapeutically productive?

DIGITAL ETHICS

This is a growth area in therapy and requires additional consideration and explanation with regard to working in an overtly ethical manner. With counselling no longer always being face-to-face, our contracting must be designed to accommodate the methodologies we employ. However, there is also a need to ensure that we only cover relevant detail and in a style that is accessible for clients without being patronising. It can be difficult to word in such a way that is clearly understood to all and not overly technical. If we are trained to deliver online therapy (synchronous or asynchronous) our contract should be different to that of a service that offers telephone work. Clients may well require very clear explanations of any synchronous and asynchronous working practices if they aren't sure of the implications of each. Other aspects to reflect on include:

1. Do you have a presence on Facebook or other social media platforms?
2. If a client does an online search for you, what will they find?
3. Do you post accessible personal details such as family photos online?
4. What would you do if a current client sent you a 'friend' request on Facebook?
5. What would you do if a former client sent you a 'friend' request on Facebook?
6. Have you ever been tempted to 'Google' clients?
7. Do you integrate appropriate apps into your therapy?
8. If so, where are the boundaries of therapeutic responsibility and how is this communicated to your clients?
9. Do you offer VOIP sessions such as Skype and FaceTime and how is this covered within your contract in respect of confidentiality, storage, privacy, etc.?
10. Are sessions recorded and saved anywhere?
11. How can you guarantee security and confidentiality of session content?
12. Does your storage arrangement adhere to the Data Protection law of the country you are practising in?

HOW RISKS TO THE THERAPEUTIC RELATIONSHIP MIGHT BE AVOIDED

We should always be aware of risks to our client and risks to ourselves and avoid those that are unethical, dangerous or unprofessional. That said, no successful practice will be risk free as an element of planned risk can be necessary to challenge and motivate ourselves and our client. What is deemed safe and what is not is determined by our ethical decision-making processes. According to Davies (2015) *'Ethical decision making is the practical process through which clinicians or counsellors base their actions, behaviour and choices on informed, sound judgement. It draws on values, principles and standards of behaviour that inform professional practice.'* What we should be aiming to avoid are risks to the therapeutic relationship itself. Situations such as moving a client to a next stage, encouraging change and experimenting with new strategies could all be classed as risky from a therapeutic perspective, but are still necessary for progress. There are some fundamental strategies that can help foster a supportive and trusting alliance.

1. Place the client at the centre of what we do.
2. Ask the client about their experience of the therapeutic relationship.
3. Remain honest, open and warm.
4. If a client is unhappy, explain what is happening and why.
5. Refer back to the original contract and re-negotiate if necessary.
6. Maintain encouraging communication, even if the relationship is under strain.

A key aspect underpinning this process is respecting the client's world view and value base and acknowledging that it is as important to them as ours is to us. We should focus on developing skills and methods to balance both theirs and ours in a professional manner that supports both. This can be challenging if the alliance is under strain or ruptured but here, the support and guidance from your supervisor is crucial. Returning to the contract can also help as a therapeutic tool if your client is looking for some tangible change.

AREAS OF CONCERN AND POTENTIAL CHALLENGES

There are many areas of working through and agreeing a contract that can be challenging for both counsellor and client. We have already touched on some, but the counsellor may well find the concept of shared control in this negotiating process daunting as it involves the implicit trust of a new, unknown client. The uncertainty felt by a client who hasn't experienced this process before can also come as an unexpected hurdle to both. Due to the unique dynamic of the therapeutic encounter, everyone's concerns are going to potentially lie in different places with different clients. To avoid confusion, consider how you can check that your client has understood the agreement and allow the client to question and clarify without patronising them.

Think of five areas of your current practice that you have concerns about or find challenging. Using the information we have covered so far, identify three steps you can take for each to reduce your concern. It is important to keep evidence of your dynamic ethical decision making (rather than a simple binary good or bad, yes or no) as it may be necessary to produce if issues arise in the future. Bear in mind that we can't use the excuse of the client giving us permission to be unethical in our professional working. As independent, autonomous professionals we are wholly responsible for our own decisions and boundaries.

Questions for reflection

Here are some questions which you might take to clinical supervision or discuss with colleagues in relation to you and your organisation's current boundaries:

1. Is our current way of contracting in line with current legislation?
2. Is the way we contract meeting the needs of our clients?
3. Is the way I contract meeting the needs of myself?
4. Is the way we contract meeting the needs of my organisation?
5. Is the way we contract meeting the requirements of the counselling profession?
6. In what areas would I benefit from further professional development?

Chapter summary

The more thorough, transparent and agreed the contract, the less risk there is of a client being confused by or unhappy with the service provided. Providing the client with relevant information and offering some choice regarding their sessions can be empowering and a formative stage of the therapeutic process. Providing a document of the agreed contract (paper or electronic) allows the client to refer to it when they choose, reinforces that it's a working document and increases a sense of ownership. Some element of measured risk is necessary to successful therapy but not regarding the therapeutic relationship.

FURTHER READING

Reeves, A. (2015). *Working with risk in counselling and psychotherapy.* London: Sage.

Sills, C. (ed.) (2006). *Contracts in counselling and psychotherapy.* London: Sage.

Van Rijn, B. (2015). *Assessment and case formulation in counselling and psychotherapy.* London: Sage.

HOLDING CONFIDENTIALITY

Along with safe, ethical practice and appropriate use of skills, confidentiality is a cornerstone of therapeutic practice. Issues surrounding confidentiality are plentiful and managing the accompanying pressures can be daunting. Potential conflicts involving confidentiality can arise in any routine practice when working alone, within teams or in assessing client risk. In this chapter we will consider the concept of professional discretion and reflect on how the limits of confidentiality can vary within different settings and some of the implications this can have for our therapeutic practice. We will also focus on legal issues relating to data protection and our rights and responsibilities with respect to requests from police and courts for counsellors' notes. In addition to considering the impact boundaries of confidentiality can have on our clients and relevant external bodies, we will reflect on the impact that holding confidentiality can have on counsellors and psychotherapists, their need for support and self-care and how to remain safe.

CONFIDENTIALITY AS A CORNERSTONE OF THERAPEUTIC PRACTICE

Confidentiality is a core aspect of the therapeutic relationship. The concept and practice of clearly defined limits to privacy is difficult to find in other aspects of life. Knowing that the content of sessions remains within the agreed boundaries of the counselling contract brings a safety and trust that is necessary for psychological growth to take place. Rogers (1961: 50) referred to this as an '*outer condition of trustworthiness'* within person-centred therapy which, when interwoven with honesty and congruence is a foundation for the therapeutic process. The safety of confidentiality facilitates the development of a range of trust connections that are necessary for other counselling processes to take place.

- Clearly defined limits to confidentiality allows the client to trust the counsellor and their relationship.
- The safety found in known limits allows the client to trust the counselling process and ultimately for them to trust themselves.
- A parallel process also takes place whereby the counsellor is able to trust the client and in turn the therapeutic alliance, counselling process and them self.

Rogers (1961: 69) articulated this by writing as if he were the client experiencing therapy, '*Maybe this is what it means to be me. But of course I can only do this because I feel safe in the relationship with my therapist.*' By this he explained that the boundaries that allow trust also allow the client to experiment with being true to them self and potentially, with others. If a client is unsure of what they can and can't say and of what might or might not be passed on, they are unlikely to trust the relationship sufficiently to allow themselves to be vulnerable. Trusting strong boundaries offers a freedom to be oneself.

DIFFERING TYPES OF CONFIDENTIALITY

Developing strong boundaries requires being explicit when discussing and agreeing confidentiality. A client might understand the concept of confidentiality differently to us so the inclusion of examples can be helpful to clarify exactly what we mean by our limits. In Chapter 1 we acknowledged that some boundaries are externally set and therefore inflexible but our clients should be aware of exactly what that means to them in the dynamic of the therapeutic alliance. While some agencies advertise a '*confidential counselling*' service clients will understandably expect completely confidential counselling even if this isn't strictly the case. We have a responsibility to represent our legal and professional boundaries accurately so clients are totally aware that there are some situations where we can or must break confidentiality. These are

- When the client consents.
- Where it is *required* by law.
- Where it is *allowed* by law.

Clearly, our client consenting to sharing information is the desired option but, unfortunately that is not always the case. If we feel that the level of risk is such that we must share client information and are unsure of our responsibilities, supervision is vital for clarification and reassurance, in addition to reading agency policies and procedures. In certain situations, such as disclosure of planned terrorism the Prevention of Terrorism Act (2005) requires us to pass relevant information to the police; this is also the case with disclosed money laundering. Not to do so would result in assumed collusion.

Circumstances where we are allowed to break confidentiality tend to be in the public interest, when not sharing information would result in members of the public being at risk. An example of this might include our client choosing a method of ending their life or an action that would harm others; the focus here is on physical harm rather than psychological. The Suicide Act (1961) clearly states that ending one's life is a legal, autonomous decision unless the client could be diagnosed with a mental illness which could impede their ability to give informed consent. The onus is on the client to disclose a diagnosis of a mental health condition and the phrase 'could be' can be a source of dilemma for many counsellors. Although there is no legal duty in the UK to report concerns regarding suicide, some employers include specific requirements within their policies and procedures, for example, reporting suicidal ideation to the client's GP. Under UK law, there is also no automatic assumption that a client expressing suicidal intention is mentally ill.

With regard to our responsibilities when supporting a client at risk, the law states that aiding, abetting, counselling and procuring the suicide of another is illegal with up to 14 years in prison. Therefore it is necessary for us to balance our level of support with our appropriate options to manage our legal obligations. One of those obligations is to be able to demonstrate our decision-making process with regard to confidentiality. We may not be legally obliged to keep session notes but there is a definite advantage to being able to provide evidence of your process if it is required. According to Bond and Mitchels 'The lack of records may prevent the therapist from providing evidence ... Therefore it could make it much more likely that the therapist will have to give evidence in person' (2008: 139). Therefore, if we keep few or no notes, we may be expected to attend an inquest to explain our decision making.

This is just one example of when managing and maintaining confidentiality can test a counsellor. There are no hard and fast rules covering every eventuality which is a situation that often worries counsellors. Developing strategies based on possible situations will build confidence in knowing how and when to share content about a client at risk.

WHAT TO DO IF YOU WERE WORKING WITH A CLIENT AT RISK WITH A DISCLOSED MENTAL HEALTH CONDITION

This would be fairly straightforward as we can include our client's awareness of their health issues and any implications when negotiating our contract. However, what about working with a client at risk with an undisclosed mental health condition? Of course we wouldn't know. As we all sit somewhere on the mental health spectrum, our everyday practice should reflect that, in the same way that Universal Precautions are automatically used by medical staff with all patients; by remaining mindful of every client's mental wellbeing, their safety doesn't then depend upon disclosing a diagnosis of a mental health condition. If unsure, the Mental Capacity Act (2005) can provide guidance if you consider your client to be an adult at risk (Gov.UK, 2015). The Act applies in England and Wales if '... *a person lacks capacity in relation to a matter if at the material time he is unable to make a decision for himself in relation to the matter because of an impairment of, or disturbance in the functioning of the mind or brain*.' The equivalent in Scotland is the Adults with Incapacity (Scotland) Act (2000) and the Mental Capacity Act (Northern Ireland) (2016) in Northern Ireland. Bearing all this in mind, if our baseline is one of gentle care, we clarify our legal and ethical responsibilities and we provide every client with a safe environment, we can demonstrate safe practice.

CONFIDENTIALITY WITHIN PRIVATE PRACTICE

Our level of confidentiality depends greatly on the organisation or service in which we are working. Profit-making organisations fall into the private category but differ significantly from individuals in private practice when it comes to managing confidentiality. When working in a large organisation, paperwork and procedures are already *in situ* but in private practice, confidentiality might be agreed between the counsellor and their client. There will be exceptions to this but these will be covered in the contract. This situation is fairly straightforward if we follow the guidance provided within our professional ethical framework, policies and procedures and legislation relating to confidentiality. Our key considerations in respect of confidentiality are threefold:

- data protection
- the rights of the client
- the safety of the client.

These aspects may guide the establishing of our boundaries but within that there is a significant amount of freedom and with any freedom, comes choice. When working for ourselves, we have an additional responsibility to develop our own service policies, of which confidentiality is one. It can be considerably more daunting to develop your own documentation and here an increased level of knowledge and confidence is required. It can also be challenging knowing there isn't a colleague or team who can be consulted informally to clarify any areas of concern. Internet forums and regular supervision can be great support but they are not always immediate. If you maintain client notes and process personal information, you may have to register with the Information Commissioner's Office unless you are exempt. (See the Further Reading section at the end of this chapter for a link to the self-assessment website.)

CONFIDENTIALITY IN STATUTORY SETTINGS

The experience is significantly different as a counsellor working within the statutory sector (such as hospitals, GP surgeries, prisons, schools and local authority social care departments), where the rules regarding confidentiality are clearly defined. There may be instances where information needs to be shared with other members of the care team, such as a case conference. In this setting discretion is crucial. As mentioned in Chapter 3, during the contracting stage, the client should be made aware you may be contributing to discussions about their care with other professionals. It should also be agreed that only professionals directly involved in their care will be included and that usually, no detail is provided but general themes, trends or an overview. Even better, the client can be invited to attend in person to answer questions, express their feelings and evaluate their progress. Although not relating directly to counselling, the General Medical Council website contains some very clear advice to medical staff regarding sharing information within a healthcare team or with others providing care. This is relevant to us as counsellors as it gives us an insight into the boundaries that colleagues must adhere to. It also informs us how and why others within a care team may work with confidentiality in a very different way from us.

Sharing information within the healthcare team or with others providing care:

25. Most patients understand and accept that information must be shared within the healthcare team in order to provide their care.

You should make sure information is readily available to patients explaining that, unless they object, personal information about them will be shared within the healthcare team, including administrative and other staff who support the provision of their care.

26. This information can be provided in leaflets, posters, on websites, and face to face and should be tailored to patients' identified needs as far as practicable. Posters might be of little assistance to patients with sight impairment or who do not read English, for example. In reviewing the information provided to patients, you should consider whether patients would be surprised to learn about how their information is being used and disclosed.

27. You must respect the wishes of any patient who objects to particular information being shared within the healthcare team or with others providing care, unless disclosure would be justified in the public interest. If a patient objects to a disclosure that you consider essential to the provision of safe care, you should explain that you cannot refer them or otherwise arrange for their treatment without also disclosing that information.

28. You must make sure that anyone you disclose personal information to understands that you are giving it to them in confidence, which they must respect. All staff members receiving personal information in order to provide or support care are bound by a legal duty of confidence, whether or not they have contractual or professional obligations to protect confidentiality.

29. Circumstances may arise in which a patient cannot be informed about the disclosure of information, for example in a medical emergency. In such a case you should pass relevant information promptly to those providing the patient's care. If and when the patient is capable of understanding, you should inform them how their personal information was disclosed if it was in a way they would not reasonably expect. (GMC, 2016)

We can see from these guidelines that there are clear commonalities with our own professional and ethical guidelines as they are all underpinned by Data Protection legislation.

CONFIDENTIALITY WITHIN VOLUNTARY (OR OTHER ORGANISATIONAL) SETTINGS

Working within the boundaries of a third sector agency such as addiction services, charitable organisations or non-counselling organisations like the Samaritans can have overlaps with both private and statutory settings. Counsellors have the benefit of working within a wider organisation, with support and a structure that can provide the potential for increased autonomy and a greater freedom to shape procedures to suit the particular client group. The need to manage the pressures of confidentiality can arise in routine practice but working within an environment designed to meet the needs of particular clients can make the process of assessing risk, working in a team, being contacted by a family member, being contacted by GP or courts requesting session content slightly smoother. Systems and proformas can be designed to apply to specific circumstances such as the focus on safety in Women's Aid, gender balance in Rape Crisis or the listening service provided by Samaritans. These are freedoms in which the other sectors don't always have options.

THE CONCEPT OF PROFESSIONAL DISCRETION

As with so many aspects of counselling, privacy within sessions is a spectrum with absolute confidentiality placed at one end and full disclosure at the other. Our professional discretion sits within that spectrum.

- Confidentiality refers to not divulging personal information to third parties.
- Discretion is the power to make a decision based on the presenting facts of the current situation.
- Privacy is a right to lack of intrusion into one's personal life.

Secrecy, on the other hand, is when something is to be hidden or unknown by others and has no place in professional counselling. It often brings with it connotations of collusion. We should be very clear of the differences between these terms as we use all three concepts to maintain professional boundaries. We do this by putting the following strategies in place to keep our client at the centre of any decision:

- Clear contracting.
- Referring back to boundaries when relevant with client.
- Clarifying situations and decisions with supervisor.
- Remaining aware of current legislation.
- Conferring with colleagues if appropriate.
- Being conversant in organisational policy.

This is not and should not be an easy and straightforward process. Every situation is different and it is impossible to predict outcomes. As counsellors, we have to engage in ethical decision making and opt for the safest outcome for our client.

> Frances explained that she was worried about the safety of her children. A close family member disclosed that he was attracted to her 12-year-old daughter and wanted to access support. She admitted that she was telling the counsellor as she also wanted support whilst seeking help. How might a counsellor contain the session?

When this took place, the counsellor first asked the client what they would like to happen next. Following the session, they made an early appointment with their supervisor, discussed the situation at length with their line manager and organisational procedures, clarified the current legislation in this area and consulted their ethical guidelines. The decision to report the situation to a Social Work Helpline came directly from the client who requested to contact them herself whilst remaining in the therapy room, which she felt was a safe and contained space. The outcome was highly successful with all involved being treated with care and compassion. Six months later, the client felt the incident was firmly in her past and was able to move on.

This example demonstrates that our client is often clear about their intentions which can help greatly when trying to decide what to do with sensitive information. This information isn't always spoken, so our management of written notes and their formatting should also be considered. To be clear, session or clinical notes as process notes aren't always kept. (Process notes are an extensive and often verbatim record of the session from our own perspective and are useful in supervision or training. They must, according to data protection legislation, be destroyed as soon as they have been used for that purpose.) Session notes however are a factual record of what took place during the session and, although not legally required, increase and help our professionalism. Even writing up anonymised accounts of therapy should be included. The UKCP states that:

> 3.4 The psychotherapist commits to safeguard the welfare and anonymity of clients when any form of publication of clinical material is being considered and to always obtain their client's verifiable consent in any

case where the welfare or anonymity of a client may be compromised. This includes situations where a client or former client might recognise themselves in case material despite the changing of names or actual circumstances. (UKCP, 2009)

Here we may be drawn to the possibility of inadvertently breaking confidentiality if our anonymising isn't robust.

The storage of clients' notes is also included when considering confidentiality. Counsellors record sensitive personal information which, in the Data Protection Act (1998) includes:

- the racial or ethnic origin of the data subject
- his political opinions
- his religious beliefs or other beliefs of a similar nature
- whether he is a member of a trade union (within the meaning of the Trade Union and Labour Relations (Consolidation) Act 1992)
- his physical or mental health or condition
- his sexual life
- the commission or alleged commission by him of any offence
- any proceedings for any offence committed or alleged to have been committed by him, the disposal of such proceedings or the sentence of any court in such proceedings.

Having sensitive and personal information in our care requires us to take responsible, appropriate and professional steps to keep it confidential. Guidance for this is contained within the Act. The Data Protection Act 1998 (see Gov.UK, 2015) controls how your personal information is used by organisations, businesses or the government. Everyone responsible for using data has to follow strict rules called 'data protection principles'. They must make sure the information is:

- used fairly and lawfully
- used for limited, specifically-stated purposes
- used in a way that is adequate, relevant and not excessive
- accurate
- kept for no longer than is absolutely necessary
- handled according to people's data protection rights
- kept safe and secure
- not transferred outside the European Economic Area without adequate protection.

Using these eight principles as a foundation to underpin our practice can help us balance our legal requirements with our ethical relationship with our client.

DATA PROTECTION PRINCIPLES

Impact on counselling practice

USED FAIRLY AND LAWFULLY

We only collate relevant information on our clients and for the purpose intended. We make sure that we know exactly what information is relevant, how we intend to use and store it, who can view it and how our clients or colleagues can access it.

USED FOR LIMITED, SPECIFICALLY STATED PURPOSES

The information that we have on our client is only used in relation to our counselling practice and relationship. Our paperwork and administration systems are fit for purpose.

USED IN A WAY THAT IS ADEQUATE, RELEVANT AND NOT EXCESSIVE

Details we have on our clients is in keeping with our practice and maintains a balance between being sufficient to allow us to do our job professionally but not so detailed that we gather irrelevant information.

ACCURATE

Information should be valid and unambiguous. If we are not sure of the accuracy, we clarify that, e.g. 'the client stated that...' or 'according to...'

KEPT FOR NO LONGER THAN IS ABSOLUTELY NECESSARY

Ensure that our policy and procedure relating to the storage of client's information is in keeping with the setting in which we work. Regularly assess our method of destroying old data to ensure it remains within current secure practice.

HANDLED ACCORDING TO PEOPLE'S DATA PROTECTION RIGHTS

Keep up to date via CPD and reading to ensure that clients' current data protection rights are adhered to.

KEPT SAFE AND SECURE

All data, whether electronic or hard copies is stored in securely locked environment so only accessible to those with a right to access it.

This includes a range of measures such as password protection, encryption and lockable filing cabinets.

NOT TRANSFERRED OUTSIDE THE EUROPEAN ECONOMIC AREA WITHOUT ADEQUATE PROTECTION

If we offer counselling (via Skype for example) with clients overseas, this is an obvious aspect to assess. However, any electronic transfer of notes crossing international boundaries should be considered, so if our notes are stored in a cloud repository such as Dropbox or OneDrive, where is that situated globally?

It is interesting to reflect on who owns the content of a counselling session. If we focus on confidentiality from the perspective of the counsellor, it may differ greatly from viewing it from the perspective of the client. We could argue that the client is sharing information about their life and personal history, therefore they own the content. If they own the content, they can do with it as they choose but consider the following questions:

1. If they own the content, do they have a right to share it?
2. How might we feel if our client asked to record the session?
3. Do we feel it is appropriate or sufficiently empowered to enquire why?
4. How might we feel if we discovered our client was writing about our sessions on social media?
5. How might we feel if we found that content of our sessions had been transcribed onto the client's Facebook page?

Clearly these are simply areas to consider rather than questions with a direct answer. Whilst some counsellors may feel a sense of outrage if they discovered client's disclosure of a counselling transcript on social media, feeling that their confidentiality had been breached, others may see it as the perfect moment to discuss a renegotiation of boundaries that more meet the needs of the client. We might only spend 50 minutes a week in the company of a client but the chances are that they will continue to dwell on the content of the session for the rest of the week. The client's sharing of the session may be a core part of their therapeutic processing. Rather than viewed negatively as a betrayal, this would be the ideal opportunity to reopen discussions on confidentiality and what it means to the client. This is a chance to re-examine current boundaries and negotiate how they might work more successfully for both parties. Considering these possibilities with your counselling supervisor in advance of experiencing them would allow for a strategy to be already in place should it occur.

Dorothy met with her client Leanne for eight weekly sessions before Leanne mentioned in passing that on a number of occasions she had written about what they talked about on her Facebook page. Dorothy was taken aback as she felt that they had agreed on confidentiality during their contracting. She asked Leanne about her understanding of the level of confidentiality they had initially agreed on and Leanne was quite clear that when they first met, they had agreed that Dorothy wouldn't share the content of their sessions. This differed from Dorothy's memory as she assumed that the agreement applied to both of them. Realising that this wasn't the case, Dorothy asked Leanne if she could share her feelings about putting personal experiences on social media and explain her motivation. Leanne talked openly about how important her friends' views were to her and saw her counselling sessions as being 'like visits to the doctor'. She didn't see anything wrong in sharing what she felt was her appointment with people who mattered to her.

1. What is your initial reaction to this scenario and where might this reaction stem from?
2. Is this a situation you have found yourself in? If so, are you happy with the way you dealt with it?
3. Have you initiated a discussion with clients on their understanding of confidentiality even if they haven't mentioned it first?

There are a range of different issues it might raise with you, some of which are identified below:

1. turning a private discussion into a public one
2. fear of judgment from others
3. others interfering or influencing your work
4. vulnerability
5. betrayal by a client
6. content being taken out of your hands.

Of course, it may well be that many of our clients share content from our sessions but we don't know about it because it never appears on a public platform. The question then becomes; does the chosen audience make a difference to the way we feel? If our client talks over their session privately with their partner, do we accept it differently to if they make it more public?

LEGAL ISSUES RELATING TO DATA PROTECTION

As legislation is a dynamic and changing process, it is important we remain up to date with our knowledge. There are many sources for information, including those in the further reading section below. Authors such as Tim Bond and Peter Jenkins specialise in writing for counsellors in matters of law. In the UK, the Information Commissioner's Office is an independent body that produces clear overviews of legal rights, essentially translating legal terminology into practical guidance. They explain that information security

> means you must have appropriate security to prevent the personal data you hold being accidentally or deliberately compromised. In particular, you will need to:
>
> 1   design and organise your security to fit the nature of the personal data you hold and the harm that may result from a security breach;
> 2   be clear about who in your organisation is responsible for ensuring information security;
> 3   make sure you have the right physical and technical security, backed up by robust policies and procedures and reliable, well-trained staff; and
> 4   be ready to respond to any breach of security swiftly and effectively.
>
> (www.ico.org.uk/for-organisations/guide-to-data-protection/principle-7-security/)

As for how we retain information about clients, the ICO state:

> 1   review the length of time you keep personal data;
> 2   consider the purpose or purposes you hold the information for in deciding whether (and for how long) to retain it;
> 3   securely delete information that is no longer needed for this purpose or these purposes; and
> 4   update, archive or securely delete information if it goes out of date.
>
> (www.ico.org.uk/for-organisations/guide-to-data-protection/principle-5-retention.

They also produce checklists that can be referred to if deciding whether to share information or not. It should be noted that these are based on law and not written specifically for therapeutic settings meaning they provide legal guidelines with no reference to ethical guidelines.

When it comes to our practice, other than our note keeping, there is no law that explicitly states we have a duty of confidentiality but the courts do recognise that clients wouldn't trust us if we didn't. Therefore, we must decide on how to act in the best interests of our client and ourself within this parameter.

BREAKING CONFIDENTIALITY

There will be times when we need break confidentiality. The manner in which we approach this will determine how we maintain our therapeutic relationship. As previously explained in this chapter, this may be a result of the client being a risk to themselves, to others or in danger.

SAFEGUARDING

Although there are circumstances where the law dictates that we don't inform our client of passing on information (e.g. terrorism and drug money laundering), it is certainly recommended that we include our client in our decision-making process. By being as transparent as possible, and taking time to frame our actions so our client is aware of our care, we reduce the chance of rupturing our alliance.

IMPLICATIONS OF THIS ON OUR OWN THERAPEUTIC PRACTICE

Earlier we considered the value of a safe environment on the therapeutic alliance and the counselling process. This highlighted the necessity for our clients to be aware of confidentiality limits to facilitate any exploration and subsequent vulnerability. It is helpful to take this a step further and reflect on the potential impact our management and handling of confidential material can have on those involved. The spectrum includes complete confidentiality, counsellor's discretion and full disclosure. How might each of these:

1. Impact on client?
2. Impact on counsellor?
3. Impact on supervisor?

4. Impact on organisation?
5. Impact on team/colleagues?
6. Impact on profession?

This is a challenging exercise to conduct in supervision and can raise personal issues relating to our perception of self, power and purpose.

POLICE AND COURT REQUESTS FOR COUNSELLORS' NOTES

There are times when our records might be requested by the police or courts. If our notes are purely factual and our client is aware of the content and consents to their release, there is little to cause concern. However, it is rarely that straightforward and as counsellors, we can experience high levels of stress in this situation. Here are some scenarios that might arise:

1. *If our client doesn't consent* when session or clinical notes are requested by a judge, we still have a legal obligation to submit them. However, by ensuring that they do not contain personal or professional assumptions or process content, the breach of confidentiality can be reduced to minimum impact. Discussing it fully with the client and allowing them access to the content demonstrates your transparency.
2. *If we are concerned about a significant breach in confidentiality*, we can offer to write a report that covers the content being requested without including superfluous details on the rest of the therapy. This alternative is often well received as the report would focus solely on the information sought.
3. *If we work within an organisation*, we should ask for guidance from our line manager and/or their legal advisors.
4. *If the police request records*, we are not required to pass them on without being subpoenaed by a judge. Although we may feel intimidated or perceived as unhelpful, we can still negotiate the best format in which to present the information. We can also include our client in this discussion.
5. *If notes for a former client are requested*, we should attempt to contact them directly. If it is not possible to contact them, we should discuss it in supervision and with our line manager or colleagues to establish the best way to balance our legal obligation with our ethical duty to our client.

THE IMPACT ON COUNSELLORS AND PSYCHOTHERAPISTS OF HOLDING CONFIDENTIALITY AND THEIR NEED FOR SUPPORT TO MAINTAIN THIS

Being approached to provide information about clients is never a pleasant experience, but there are very few situations that haven't been experienced by a counsellor before. The ability to keep the situation in proportion and maintain self-care are upmost. A key element of this is to know where to find answers if they are needed. There are additional external sources of support over and above clinical supervision. Professional bodies run helplines developed to provide general guidance as do indemnity insurance providers. There are online networks, articles in journals and websites which can offer information if not guidance. The requirement to regularly update our understanding and skills is also valid here, especially if you choose to build on your knowledge of legal responsibilities. When employed by and working for an organisation, your contract usually means that you are an agent of the employer and as such, it is the organisation that is being challenged rather than you as an individual.

To be asked to share information may be challenging but so can 'holding' information. In everyday therapy, we are privy to incredibly personal and private information and it can effect our wellbeing. A client can introduce a subject where we experience an unexpected emotional or even physical reaction. Holding information that has such an impact on us can also be challenging. Regular supervision allows us to share information about ourselves, our responses and our feelings relating to a client's story which is the main method of unloading, exploring and developing ways to deal with our reactions. We can also consider using creative methods and activities to process our holding of a client's content such as art, writing and music.

Questions for reflection

1. What does confidentiality mean to me in my practice?
2. What strategies do I have in place for support and keeping myself right?
3. How do I balance discretion with confidentiality?
4. How might you ensure that a new client has the capacity to give informed consent?

5. Am I confident regarding the legislation, policies and procedures and ethical framework that relate to my work?
6. What are my concerns in this area and how might I gain peace of mind?
7. How might you approach discussing confidentiality in the context of your fears surrounding your client's risk?

Chapter summary

Initially we should establish an unambiguous contract that is fully discussed and agreed to determine our limits to confidentiality. Our practice should have a foundation of care and as professional practitioner, we have a duty to uphold our legal and ethical responsibilities. To demonstrate best practice, every client should be provided with a detailed, signed contract and an explanation of safe boundaries.

FURTHER READING

Bond, T. (2010). *Essential law for counsellors and psychotherapists.* London: Sage.

Data Protection Act (1998). Available at: www.legislation.gov.uk/ ukpga/1998/29/contents (accessed 1 September 2016).

ICO (n.d.). Available at: www.ico.org.uk/for-organisations/register/self-assessment/ (accessed 3 September 2016).

Jenkins, P. (2007). *Counselling, psychotherapy and the law.* London: Sage.

Reeves, A. (2015). *Working with risk in counselling and psychotherapy.* London: Sage.

NAVIGATING DUAL RELATIONSHIPS

The therapeutic relationship is a professional alliance intended to support clients that we don't personally know and, usually, have never met before. There may be circumstances where we happen across our clients in another setting. This meeting, whether planned or not, will have an impact on our relationship. It can also add a layer of complexity to our therapeutic work. Because of this, there are times when dual relationships are best avoided as supporting ethical and therapeutic practice when in such a situation can become overly challenging. However, there are times when this situation might be unavoidable and we should consider how we might manage our boundaries if this were the case.

WHAT ARE DUAL RELATIONSHIPS?

There are many types of dual relationship, many are preventable but some are not. To start, we will concentrate on current clients rather than former clients. The impact of the additional meetings on the therapeutic alliance will depend on the type, level and permanence of the secondary role. There are many but the six most common are:

- Dual **social** relationships, either as a personal friendship or via online media, for example 'friends' on a social networking site other than a specific counselling site.
- Dual **institutional** relationships such as counselling staff within a military base, occupational health department or university who are also colleagues.

- Dual **community** relationships where counsellor and client/s live within a small village or town resulting in chance meetings between sessions. This is common within interdependent communities such as the deaf community where there are a limited number of counsellors.
- Dual **business** relationships where an employer/employee association is formed outside the therapy room. An example of this would be to employ a client to decorate your office. In some cultures, the exchange of business would be accepted.
- Dual **professional** relationships, e.g. working on research or a writing project with your supervisor can fall within this category. Providing evidence relating to a client in court can also introduce additional responsibilities.
- Dual **treatment** relationships often occur in addiction services where a counsellor might also facilitate relaxation, art or other therapeutic activities.

These are all direct connections, but we can also find ourselves in an unknown or unexpected, indirect dual relationship, such as discovering that a client is the partner of a colleague, or a friend of a friend. Overlaps in role are '*almost unavoidable if you are based within a rural location or are one of few local counselling services. It is unacceptable to work therapeutically with a client who you know such as a friend, colleague or family member. Because of this, issues surrounding dual relationships tend to only emerge with current or past clients – not future ones as they can't be clients if you already know them*' (Amis, 2011). In this situation, we should be open and honest with our client and disclose the link. In supervision we should consider the impact that awareness of this secondary relationship might have on the client, the therapeutic alliance and process as well as yourself. We need to assess the impact any additional relationship may have on the power balance in the counselling room and ensure we avoid causing harm or exploiting our client in any way.

A clear explanation is included within section 1.5 of the UKCP *Ethical Principles and Code of Professional Conduct* (2009):

> Psychotherapists are required to carefully consider possible implications of entering into dual or multiple relationships and make every effort to avoid entering into relationships that risks confusing an existing relationship and may impact adversely on a client. For example, a dual or multiple relationships could be a social or commercial relationship between the psychotherapist and client, or a supervisory relationship which runs alongside the therapeutic one. When dual or multiple relationships are unavoidable, for example in small communities, psychotherapists take responsibility to clarify and manage boundaries and confidentiality of the therapeutic relationship.

As with all potentially influencing factors, we should also reflect on the permanence of the situation. The spectrum includes very temporary overlaps, such as walking past each other in street, through to finding ourselves at the same party, right up to attending the same church on a regular basis or having children who attend the same school so meet daily at the gate.

If we meet a client in a public setting, it depends where it is as to what we may feel is the right thing to do. If we pass a client in the street, we might already have agreed during our contracting that we will respond if they acknowledge us first or there will be no sign of recognition. We don't want to put them in a position of having to explain who we are to anyone they are with. Meeting unexpectedly at a party can still be a temporary, single incident, but takes a greater degree of decision making. Do you leave immediately, risk appearing rude and sacrifice your evening? What if you are both attending a wedding? If drinking, do you limit your alcohol intake? What if your client were to approach you? There are a range of aspects to consider to protect the professional boundaries in a personal or social arena. It is not simply a case of agreeing what to do with your client in advance, but also who they or you might be with. Your family need to be made aware that they can't ask who a client is when you are seen greeting a 'stranger' outside the session. This is in the same way that it may be uncomfortable for your client to introduce you to their company as their counsellor. There are always appropriate solutions but it is the element of surprise that can effect how we act at the time.

Point 33 of the BACP *Ethical Framework* provides a framework for assessing the safe management of parallel relationships with clients:

> We will establish and maintain appropriate professional and personal boundaries in our relationships with clients by ensuring that:
>
> a. these boundaries are consistent with the aims of working together and beneficial to the client.
> b. any dual or multiple relationships will be avoided where the risks of harm to the client outweigh any benefits to the client.
> c. reasonable care is taken to separate and maintain a distinction between our personal and professional presence on social media where this could result in harmful dual relationships with clients.
> d. the impact of any dual or multiple relationships will be periodically reviewed in supervision and discussed with clients when appropriate. They may also be discussed with any colleagues or managers in order to enhance the integrity of the work being undertaken.

As well as dilemmas with current clients, we can find ourself in a potential dual relationship with a former client. This could happen at any time once therapy has concluded. As guidance, Point 37 of the BACP *Ethical Framework* (2015) states that:

> We recognise that conflicts of interest and issues of power or dependence may continue after our working relationship with a client, supervisee or trainee has formally ended. We will exercise caution before entering into personal or business relationships with former clients and expect to be professionally accountable if the relationship becomes detrimental to the former client or the standing of the profession.

How we exercise caution depends very much on the circumstances and should be taken to supervision. The previous American Psychological Society's *Ethical Principles for Psychologists* (2002, not the 2010 update) identified specific factors to reflect on when considering such a liaison which can be incorporated into our assessment process:

- the amount of time that has passed since the professional relationship;
- the nature, duration, and intensity of the professional relationship;
- the circumstance of termination;
- the client's history and vulnerability;
- the client's current mental status; and
- the likelihood of an adverse impact on the client.

These points are very clear and can be successfully used in supervision as a basis for assessment of current and future relationships. Informal referrals and recommendations by former clients should be mentioned here as there is a similar evaluation process required to assess whether it is appropriate to work with the new client. There is a risk that the relationship could be compromised by both knowing the referee.

THE IMPACT OF DUAL RELATIONSHIPS ON POWER AND CONSENT

A dual professional relationship (such as counsellor and colleague) is common and not always detrimental to the counselling. It often occurs within a range of settings, such as education, where staff counselling is available in-house. Other organisations may have an occupational health department that employs counsellors. In this case, the service will usually have a policy stipulating recommendations and guidelines, or alternatively, there may be other counsellors within the team who can advise if any challenges arise. In many cases, this situation is advantageous to the therapeutic relationship as in-house

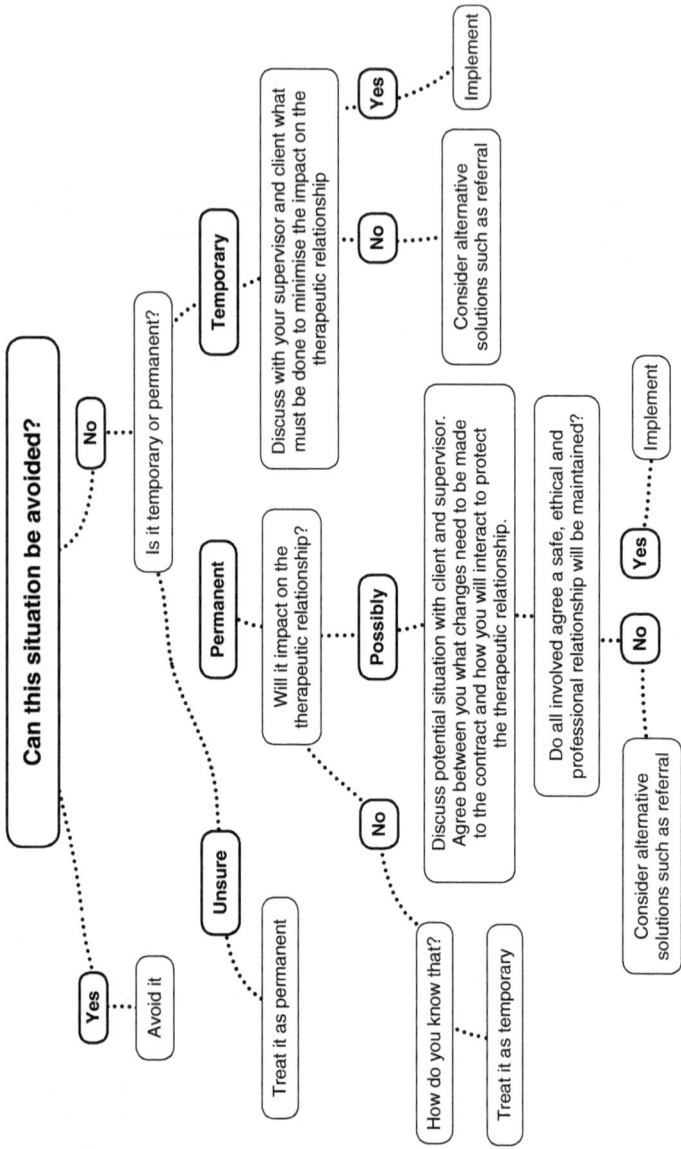

Can this situation be avoided?

- **Yes** ⋯ Avoid it
- **No** ⋯ Is it temporary or permanent?
  - **Temporary** ⋯ Discuss with your supervisor and client what must be done to minimise the impact on the therapeutic relationship
    - **Yes** ⋯ Implement
    - **No** ⋯ Consider alternative solutions such as referral
  - **Permanent** ⋯ Will it impact on the therapeutic relationship?
    - **Possibly** ⋯ Discuss potential situation with client and supervisor. Agree between you what changes need to be made to the contract and how you will interact to protect the therapeutic relationship.
      - Do all involved agree a safe, ethical and professional relationship will be maintained?
        - **Yes** ⋯ Implement
        - **No** ⋯ Consider alternative solutions such as referral
    - **No** ⋯ Treat it as temporary
  - **Unsure** ⋯ Treat it as permanent
    - **How do you know that?**

Figure 5.1

counsellors will have a greater understanding of the organisation's culture and ethos and are able to grasp the context of the workplace. Issues can arise for example, if a counsellor is working with a member of staff who is mentioned by another client or finding they're next to each other in the queue at lunchtime. As long as situations such as this have been pre-empted in the initial contracting, consent-wise it should lower the risk of future challenges. The balance of power may also be more evenly shared in this situation; both parties in the relationship are employees and so there is an externally determined equality. This equality can inform and reinforce the sense of shared power at the contracting stage. Clients have the advantage of experience within the organisations so some policies and procedures may already apply, making the context and reasons behind any challenges slightly easier to explain and understand.

It is far less predictable if a dual relationship potentially crosses the personal and professional domains and this can be more problematic. Depending on the situation, there may be areas of ethical dubiety that should be considered to maintain a professional balance in the relationship. Unlike the previous scenario, there may not be a team of colleagues on hand to support any decision so any situation may have to be initially processed alone and later reflected on with the help of your supervisor. In Chapter 3 the need to include the possibility of situations arising in the future in the contract was highlighted but, as the contract is a working document, it can be revisited at any time.

When taking the relationship outside of the therapy room, there is an opportunity for power, or the abuse of it, to be wielded by either counsellor and/or client. There may be fears surrounding manipulation, collusion or reduced confidentiality, but as long as these are openly discussed in a positive and transparent way, a healthy balance can be maintained. We should be clear that any additional meeting is not based on our own needs and that our client remains at the centre of any decision making. A key question to ask yourself is 'Can this situation be avoided and if not, what must I do to maintain a safe therapeutic environment'?

THE COMPLEXITY AND IMPLICATIONS FOR THERAPEUTIC WORK

A fundamental aim is to avoid the therapeutic relationship being compromised. This results in our need to examine any shift from a range of perspectives. Bond's model of ethical decision making (2010: 227–238) is very helpful here to provide structure (see Chapter 8). Reflecting on questions such as, 'What might this mean to my client?', 'What might this mean to me?' and 'What would my supervisor/tutor/colleague do in this situation?' can be very helpful in this process. Asking what is appropriate doesn't simply help us identify any overlapping personal and professional relationships, but also overlapping professional roles. Establishing and collating resources to consult for guidance or clarification is also helpful. This adds confidence to our decision-making process and can even indicate if this dual relationship is appropriate or even therapeutically helpful. The implications for our work might include unspoken self-disclosure.

Attending a particular social group or religious service might tell the client more about ourselves than we intended. In this instance, pre-planning how to approach it in the next counselling session can reduce potential issues. It also offers the opportunity for our client to ask questions so we are not mis-represented, they are not jumping to conclusions and it lessens the chance of assumed friendship. Instead, obviously depending on the context, it might make us appear more human and approachable. To not mention it at all would be very strange and a client might understandably question why.

Whatever the decision, one boundary that should remain inflexible is therapeutic content only being discussed during the planned session, not if you meet unexpectedly and not by text or email.

What would you do in the following situations?

1. Sandra has been attending weekly counselling sessions for seven months. She is still quite vulnerable but shared with you that she feels very safe during the sessions which is demonstrated by her level of honesty. Two months ago she admitted that she is questioning her sexuality and has been having an affair with her friend Barbara. You are attending your cousin's wedding, and notice that Sandra is also a guest. She comes over and introduces you to her husband, her friend Barbara and Barbara's husband.

2. Tom is a new client and after his third session invites you to his retirement party. He is adamant that he wants you to attend and becomes quite insistent. When you politely decline, he looks very upset.

3. Neelum has talked at length of her husband's violence towards her and their children. This week you notice she has a new, large bruise on her face and is walking with a limp. You worry for her safety and she admits that she wants to leave him as she thinks she is in danger. She knows there is a women's refuge close by but she is too scared to go on her own. She tells you that she won't go there unless you go with her and her children.

These three situations all overstep the traditional boundaries of the counsellor/client relationship. What were the influencing factors that determined your response to each? Bear in mind the balance of power, informed consent, the ethical implications and the potential impact on your therapeutic work.

Although written for psychologists rather than counsellors, the BPS *Statement of Ethics and Conduct* (2009) states that:

> i) In making decisions on what constitutes ethical practice, psychologists will need to consider the application of technical competence and the use of their professional skill and judgement. They should also be mindful of the importance of fostering and maintaining good professional relationships with clients and others as a primary element of good practice.

This final sentence reinforces the maintenance of the relationship with clients as a key consideration and illustrates that other professionals can also find themselves in similar situations. The ethical guidelines for psychologists, social workers and other care professionals are very similar in valuing the safety and boundaries of the relationship.

However, in some settings and indeed, some theoretical modalities, dual *activities* within roles are encouraged. This is the case in CBT if the therapist also supports a client outside the therapy room. Using relaxation techniques or supporting an agoraphobic client during a walk in the park would fall within this category. Alternatively, a counsellor working in a hospital may implement a direct referral which could involve elements of advocacy, information giving, advice or recommendation. This would be inappropriate in many therapeutic settings but can be part of the counsellor's role within the NHS.

WHEN DUAL RELATIONSHIPS ARE BEST AVOIDED

It is recommended to adopt an absolutist approach when a dual relationship might be deemed unethical, illegal or unsafe. Situations to avoid without exception include a sexual relationship with a current or former client, and borrowing or lending money; these are never appropriate nor ethical and should always be avoided. If unprofessional relationships are allowed to develop and ethical boundaries compromised, we would not be able to demonstrate safe practice and we would no longer be covered by our indemnity insurance. The therapeutic alliance would rupture, over-familiarity would develop and the professional relationship would be undermined and irreparable.

OVERSTEPPING PROFESSIONAL RELATIONSHIPS

Dilemmas regarding dual relationships aren't always linked to our clients. Consider the following two situations:

> 1) Six years ago Sarah was a fellow student on your training course and you were always very impressed by how accomplished she was at demonstrating counselling skills. You got on well and kept in touch. Yesterday she emailed you to tell you that she started a supervisor's course and is looking for supervisees with which to gain experience. She asks you if you would be interested as she knows that you are currently looking for a new supervisor.

What would your response be to Sarah's offer? What informed your decision-making process?

> 2) Yesterday you attended an interview for a post as counsellor for a small, local charity. At the end of the interview, you asked for clarification on their policy regarding clinical supervision. They told you that they provide it in-house; one hour of supervision after every eight sessions with Bob, your new line manager. Today they phoned you and offered you the job.

How do you respond to their provision of supervision? How do you explain to them the reasons behind this?

From these scenarios it is possible to see that the need for clear boundaries within our professional relationships stretch beyond that of client work. We need to be clear about any ethical and moral dubiety in all aspects of our work, including training, supervision and colleagues. We can develop simple strategies to support our ethical and therapeutic practice when dual relationships might be unavoidable. Introducing collaborative working relationships such as supervision, online professional support networks and knowledgeable colleagues can stand us in good stead for sourcing advice should we require it.

HOW TO SUPPORT ETHICAL AND THERAPEUTIC PRACTICE WHEN A DUAL RELATIONSHIP IS UNAVOIDABLE

When we do find ourselves in a situation where we have to manage safe dual relationships, we will most likely find ourselves working with clients who are also colleagues. With constant monitoring, assessment and reflection, we can ensure that we only occasionally cross boundaries rather than seriously violating them. It is possible to make sure that dual institutional relationship isn't exploitative or inappropriate. There may be a heightened risk of collusion but, as previously mentioned, there are certain advantages to developing a safe working practice with clients with whom we share some external influences. Discussing the potential overlaps in the relationship with our client and agreeing a shared strategy to maintain boundaries is a positive step to strengthen the alliance.

We may also find that there is potential for relational boundary ruptures online. Clients may well use your counselling service website as a means of contact but, as long as it is well structured for that purpose and there is no personal content, it is unlikely there will be an issue. One area in which to exercise caution is when writing your personal biography and/or professional history. It can be challenging to include sufficient appropriate detail whilst taking care not to over-share.

AREAS FOR CONCERN AND POTENTIAL CHALLENGES

This whole chapter has focused solely on possible areas of concern, but the crux of any potential dilemma involving dual relationships is: how do you decide when a boundary is being temporarily crossed to sustain a positive working relationship; or when a relationship is unsafe and violating professional boundaries? The answer may never be straightforward but rather dependent on a range of internal and external influences in addition to the organisational setting. There are many, similar professions where relationships are successfully managed, some with very clear boundaries, such as a GP, and others with less formal boundaries, such as a home carer. All have strategies in place for dealing with challenges to relational boundaries. We should be clear about any associated implications and be creative, flexible yet careful with possible solutions. Regular supervision is crucial as is being comfortable to be open with your client making them aware of any problematic situation. By demonstrating ethical practice your client is less likely to interpret any resistance from you as rejection.

Questions for reflection

1. Daniel was a client of yours a year ago when you worked together for 15 sessions. You have just read in the paper that he has died and his funeral is tomorrow. Will you attend? What are the considerations for and against attending?
2. Is there a situation where you would give a client a non-sexual hug?
3. Would you ever give a client a token gift at the end of your time working together?
4. Have you ever given a client a birthday card? Why?
5. How would you respond to a client approaching you outside the session?

Chapter summary

Dual relationships can be preventable but not always. They can be permanent or temporary and can help or hinder the therapeutic alliance. They can also be formal or informal depending upon the circumstances. Maintaining a parallel relationship with a client isn't automatically damaging as there can be benefits. Being guided by our ethical guidelines is key to avoiding boundary violations that are unsafe.

FURTHER READING

Kahn, M. (1997). *Between therapist and client: the new relationship.* New York: St. Martin's Press.

Lazarus, A., & Zur, O. (eds) (2002). *Dual relationships and psychotherapy.* New York: Springer Publishing Company.

Syme, G. (2003). *Dual relationships in counselling and psychotherapy: exploring the limits.* London: Sage.

KEEPING CLEAR AND SAFE SEXUAL BOUNDARIES

The ability to identify sexual dynamics and the confidence to then bring our observations or suspicions into the counselling relationship may be discomforting to face, but are necessary if we are to remain congruent. There may be situations in which attraction is communicated by the client, but there may also be times when we, as the counsellor, feel an attraction to our client. This is not an unusual occurrence. It is also possible for a similar situation to develop between supervisor and supervisee. Sexual boundaries don't end with attraction, but can also incorporate the use and interpretation of physical touch, and to some extent, the limits to our self-disclosure. In addition to our inter-relational and intra-relational dynamics, it is particularly important to be consciously aware of working ethically with clients who are survivors of sexual abuse. To engage successfully, it is helpful to develop a framework of working with sexual issues within safe, appropriate and clear boundaries.

IDENTIFYING SEXUAL DYNAMICS AND WORKING WITH THEM THERAPEUTICALLY

The nature of therapy is such that if successful, it generates a close relationship where trust is established and the disclosure of private thoughts and feelings is encouraged. This can be easily misconstrued by some clients, and indeed, some counsellors, as a personal rather than professional closeness. This situation was recognised at the very inception of counselling when Freud '... *cautioned against the seductive power of the erotic transference, where the patient may express erotic feelings or behaviour towards the analyst and the need for the latter to abstain from reciprocating in professionally inappropriate ways*' (Yakeley, 2014: 31). At the time, Freud was very concerned about his contemporaries and their flagrant disregard to recognising professional limits to their therapeutic relationships. It was common practice at the time to analyse friends and family and there were cases of psychoanalysts having sexual relationships with their clients. When writing in 1912, he was very clear in his guidance to others:

> I cannot advise my colleagues too urgently to model themselves during psychoanalytic treatment on the surgeon, who puts aside all his feelings, even as human sympathy, and concentrates his mental forces on the single aim of performing the operation as skillfully as possible. (Freud, 1912)

Despite counselling being a far more relational experience than surgery, the emergence of attraction is unpredictable and can occur unexpectedly. The clarity and reinforcement of strong boundaries helps in reducing the likelihood of any subsequent confusion. Sexual dynamics can be at play in any counselling setting and as mentioned above, are not restricted to the client. Counsellors can also feel an attraction to their client, whether that be of a physical nature or being drawn to their personality. Ethical guidelines are very clear that it is not in any way appropriate to further develop this attraction but, as part of the therapeutic relationship, we have a responsibility to acknowledge and address it.

PITFALLS AND DANGERS FOR CLIENTS AND COUNSELLORS

What constitutes sexual dynamics covers a wide spectrum ranging from the obvious to the unconscious and can be present for client, or counsellor, or both. Situations might include indirect communication involving fantasy and erotic transference or more overt behaviours such as flirtation, touch and suggestion. An active response such as reciprocation is totally unethical and absolutely forbidden but unfortunately, inappropriate dynamics can also evolve from a passive response, where we might choose to ignore our suspicions or just feel flattered.

To avoid the associated pitfalls, we should be addressing the situation appropriately by recognising what we think is happening and then bringing it from a perceived personal relationship, which doesn't exist, into the therapeutic relationship, which does. As soon as any overstepping of the professional relationship is noticed or even suspected, we have an ethical responsibility to raise our observations or concerns with our client, enabling us to work through the situation together in a manner that strengthens our alliance. By developing the range of personal topics we are able to discuss, we are both promoting a shared agenda and working with the relationship in the here and now.

Rather than appearing uncomfortable or embarrassed, this subject should be gently approached but in a manner that is matter of fact. By framing a simple question to establish the truth, we allow the client to see the possibility of discussing any feelings within the room without either judgment or rejection. Avoiding directness often takes us into a place where we are not sure of our client's true thoughts and feelings and we aren't then able to work at the relational depth necessary. An additional complication when not dealing with the situation is of it escalating into a more challenging scenario, with our client mistakenly thinking that their feelings are reciprocated. However uneasy or awkward the situation may make us feel, it can become considerably worse if left unexplored.

Any underlining motivation for the attraction may also be explored. Freud provided an example from his own experience in *Studies in Hysteria* (1895: 303–304) when he introduced the concept of transference for the first time.

> The transference on to the doctor occurs by means of a false connection. I should probably give an example here: the origin of a particular hysterical symptom in one of my patients was a wish that she had felt many years previously and immediately relegated to her unconscious, namely that the man she was talking to at the time would just take swift and firm action and give her a kiss. Once, after the end of a session, a wish like this arose in my patient with regard to myself. She is horrified about it, spends a sleepless night, and the next time, although she does not refuse treatment, is quite unfit for the work. … Now that I have experienced this once, I can assume that whenever I am involved personally in this way, a transference and false connection have again occurred.

The concept of a 'false connection' is still accurate as both client and counsellor only know each other in a role, showing a particular side of themselves: the client in the role of 'client' and the counsellor demonstrating professional skills and interactions that they wouldn't necessarily use in personal interactions.

ATTRACTION FROM CLIENT

There are several issues to reflect on from the perspective of a client expressing an attraction for their counsellor because there are many different types of attraction which can be communicated in a range of ways; some of these are innocent, others not so. As with many aspects of behaviour, there is a spectrum of clues that may indicate attraction, which ranges from the very subtle to the blatantly obvious. Examples might include a client who is attracted to our friendship, or one who may copy what we do or what we wear; they may bring us gifts or follow us (either physically or online). Having a suspicion requires clarification as clearly there has been a trigger that has caused the suspicion in the first place. It may well be nothing, a mixed signal, but it may not. Being the first to bring the subject up allows the client an opportunity to express themselves which can be facilitated in a wholly non-threatening way. We might begin with a general approach asking *'In our first session we discussed our roles and our relationship. Now that we are four weeks in, I'm wondering how this is going for you? Are you finding the way we work together is helping?'* By keeping the question open, it allows the client to focus on the working relationship. If this is not specific enough to address your suspicions, a question such as *'I notice that you are smiling at me a lot today. Is there a reason for this?'*

By basing our question on an observation or evidence, the client can see that we are picking up on their verbal and non-verbal communication and giving them a space to share their feelings. If, however, we find ourselves in a situation where a client openly declares that they are attracted to us, we should have a strategy in place to respond appropriately. Our responses need to be less general and more specific so that we approach the situation head on, not leaving room for miscommunication or misunderstanding. We should also be careful that whilst possibly feeling flattered, we do not fall into the trap of responding to our client in a way that they interpret as evidence of a deeper relationship. It would be easy but irresponsible to just remain polite and ignore the fact that such an overstepping of boundaries is neither safe nor therapeutic.

Whilst we reflect on the 'how' we raise the subject of attraction with our client, we should also be aware of the subsequent impact it may have upon our therapeutic relationship. Having a strategy in place to handle the situation sensitively ensures that the dialogue can be integrated into the therapeutic progress, rather than create a barrier to it. Even if this is a situation you are yet to find yourself in, we have a professional responsibility to plan how we might respond to and manage a declaration of attraction. In some settings, it is common to be on the receiving end of sexualised behaviours. These might include the use of suggestive words and phrases, inappropriate touch, conscious and unconscious flirting or overt offers of a sexual nature. Responses to these should still be polite but firm and refer back to the agreed relationship in the contract. It can also be helpful to identify this with your client and use the contract as a basis for discussion. Looking at the motivation behind such overt behaviour can inform us as to how we can both then work with it therapeutically. It can offer an opportunity to explore an area of the client's world that we might otherwise miss.

The following are all actual quotes from counsellors in supervision sessions. How might you respond to the following client statements?

- 'I wish I could talk to my wife the way I can talk to you.'
- 'I really look forward to seeing you each week.'
- 'I love your style. I wish I could always look as good as you do.'
- 'When you look at me like that, it makes me imagine that we have a very different kind of relationship.'
- 'We should carry on this discussion over a glass of wine.'

1. Did any make you feel uncomfortable, embarrassed or unsure as to how you might respond?
2. How comfortable would you be picking up on the statement and exploring it with your client?
3. How might you ensure that you remain professional and work within your ethical boundaries?
4. Can you pinpoint any specific areas that make you particularly uncomfortable?

Each of the statements are complimentary, but very much open for interpretation. Some appropriate responses might include:

- Accepting any intended compliment.
- Asking them to expand that thought as a means to gain clarity and intention.
- Sensitively reminding the client of the relational boundaries agreed within the contract.

Exploration shouldn't be avoided through fear or discomfort as an honest discussion is the quickest method to establish what the client is communicating, what is meant and how it relates to their current experience. Opening up the subject, rather than avoiding it, increases the likelihood that underpinning thoughts, feelings and reactions may be unearthed that will enhance the therapeutic relationship rather than detract from it.

From a theoretical rather than a practical viewpoint, the issues of transference might be considered here: the unconscious projection of a previous relationship onto a current one, i.e. that of the counsellor. The idealisation of the counsellor is a common phenomenon whereby the client sees the counsellor almost as a guru figure; a source of knowledge, expertise and answers that they find alluring. To maintain a healthy therapeutic relationship, this can be examined and used as a contributing factor to the growth and development of both the interpersonal relationship and the therapy.

ATTRACTION FROM THE COUNSELLOR

The main issue of attraction that we'll consider in this context is sexual attraction, as this situation is more common than we might think. In 2001, Giovazolias and Davis conducted a survey of registered counselling psychologists in the UK and of the 122 respondents, 95 (77.9%) disclosed that they had experienced attraction to at least one client, whereas only 27 (22.1%) had never been attracted to a client. Interestingly, of the 95 who had felt attraction towards a client, 50.5% felt it had a positive impact on the therapy, 43.2% felt it had no impact and only 6.3% reported a negative impact. This certainly suggests that we shouldn't automatically dismiss exploring the feelings honestly and transparently without giving it closer consideration. If we refer back to the main tenet of safe therapy, which is to put our client first, it will help guide our decisions as to how to approach this discussion in a manner that will add to the relationship rather than detract from it.

There is a substantive body of literature covering this phenomenon; it is even possible to trace the establishment of time limits governing when counsellors were allowed (or not) to pursue a relationship with an ex-client. Hermann and Robinson-Kurpius (2006) published an article in *Counseling Today* where they identified some specific guidelines in America:

> In the 1995 code, the specified period of waiting was two years, with extensive justification after two years that such a relationship would not be harmful to the former client. The 2005 code extends this period to five years. Echoing the previous code, the 2005 code states in Standard A.5.b. that 'Counselors, before engaging in sexual or romantic interactions or relationships with clients, their romantic partners or client family members after 5 years following the last professional contact, demonstrate forethought and document (in written form) whether the

interactions or relationship can be viewed as exploitive in some way and/or whether there is still potential to harm the former client; in cases of potential exploitation and/or harm, the counselor avoids entering such an interaction or relationship.'

This becomes even clearer in Section A5c of the 2014 update which states that:

Sexual and/or romantic counselor–client interactions or relationships with former clients, their romantic partners, or their family members are prohibited for a period of 5 years following the last professional contact. This prohibition applies to both in-person and electronic interactions or relationships. Counselors, before engaging in sexual and/or romantic interactions or relationships with former clients, their romantic partners, or their family members, demonstrate forethought and document (in written form) whether the interaction or relationship can be viewed as exploitive in any way and/or whether there is still potential to harm the former client; in cases of potential exploitation and/or harm, the counselor avoids entering into such an interaction or relationship.

However, in the UK, the BACP guidelines are rather more succinct:

1. We will not have sexual relationships with or behave sexually towards our clients, supervisees or trainees.
2. We will avoid having sexual relationships with or behaving sexually towards people whom we know to be close to our clients in order to avoid undermining our clients' trust in us.
3. We will not exploit or abuse our clients in any way: financially, emotionally, physically, sexually or spiritually.

This indicates that to develop a personal relationship with a client introduces issues of exploitation and abuse; exploitation of any vulnerability and power imbalance and abuse of our professional status.

ATTRACTION WITHIN SUPERVISION

It is recognised that the parallel relationship with our clinical supervisor can mimic the relationship we have with our clients. All the issues that can arise with the counselling sessions can appear within the supervisee/supervisor relationship. Again, it might be uncomfortable, but being honest and explaining how you feel means you can both work with any undercurrents and implications. This situation can be more straightforward to deal with as you, in the role of supervisee/ client, are aware of the dynamic and the implications. Following any discussion, an informed, joint decision can be made as to whether

- it is possible to continue working together as before
- the relationship might improve following such honesty
- it would be more appropriate to find a different supervisor.

It is common to choose a supervisor who is more experienced than ourselves, and as such, they may well be more aware of any inappropriate attraction or unspoken tension than we realise.

BOUNDARIES OF PHYSICAL TOUCH

Progressing on from the relationship, when we talk of touch within counselling, it isn't necessarily within a sexual context. There are several instances when touch might occur and most are intended to be innocent. Consider your response to these questions.

1. Do you shake hands when you meet a new client?
2. How do you respond to a crying client?
3. What would you do if a client asked for a hug?
4. Would you touch your client as a way of demonstrating reassurance?
5. Would you hug a client at the end of their final session?

Hopefully, in answering these questions it raised for you issues surrounding how a client may feel if we did or didn't use touch. Whether touch is appropriate or not depends upon your theoretical orientation, your method of practice, the relationship you have with your client and the setting you are working in. A very tactile client might feel rejected if their touch isn't reciprocated but another might be incredibly uncomfortable at the thought of a hug. In addition to personal responses, there are several risks associated with using touch. Whilst we may intend our touch to be supportive or encouraging, our client can misconstrue or misinterpret our meaning. Even innocent touch with no sexual connotation isn't always appropriate. A client attending with issues surrounding physical contact or hygiene might find it highly off-putting if a counsellor even shook their hand on their first meeting. When a client touches us in a way that we feel is inappropriate, or makes us uncomfortable, we should consider what they are communicating, why they are expressing it in that manner and how we might respond. We are aiming for a kind response whilst letting them know that it is inappropriate. There is no right or wrong here; it is an area where the counsellor must use their own discretion. The client's cultural background can influence their level of comfort with touch and physical proximity and, if it differs from ours, can cause mis-communication. Counsellors working within a hospice environment may have a very different approach to touch than a counsellor working in a medical or educational setting. The age and gender of both client and counsellor can have an impact on the perception of touch, espe-cially if those involved are comfortable with very different norms and values. The modality being worked with can also have a significant effect on how sexualised contact is received; a psychoanalyst may high-light any advances within their analysis of the client, using them to contribute to the therapy. On the other hand, a CBT practitioner may ignore it so as not to risk any reinforcement.

THERAPIST SELF-DISCLOSURE

The appropriateness and use of self-disclosure falls within the auspices of maintaining sexual boundaries. By intentionally or unintentionally over-sharing, or sharing inappropriate information, our client can then place themselves in our personal world. Telling another personal infor-mation can be a very intimate act, and as such, can be deemed as overstepping a boundary. Where we draw the line between private and personal is also a consideration. To help provide a framework to assess whether any disclosure is appropriate, Stewart (2005: 449) highlights that to disclose requires us to anticipate:

- our own feelings
- the other person's reactions
- the possible effect on the relationship.

If we feel that the disclosure is helpful to the client and not motivated by our own needs, it may well be appropriate. In fact, there are many uses for such connections: Egan (2013: 185–186) felt this to be the case when he includes self-disclosure into Stage 2 of his helping model as a therapeutic tool. He provides the following guidelines:

- Make sure that your disclosures are appropriate.
- Make sure that disclosures are culturally appropriate.
- Be careful of your timing.

- Keep your disclosure selective and focused.
- Don't disclose too frequently.
- Do not burden the client.
- Remain flexible.

To illustrate the impact of sharing on a very personal level, Moore and Jenkins (2012) conducted a study focusing on disclosing sexual orientation to clients and identified key themes that emerged from their research. These included the counsellor's fear of client judgment, a need for therapist self-protection, self-awareness of the potential impact of their own fears and prejudices on the therapeutic relations and the potential relevance of internalised homophobia. Their conclusion was that a gay or lesbian counsellor disclosing their sexual orientation to a straight client is potentially problematic and risky. This study concentrated on intentional disclosure, and due to the very private nature of the disclosure, the findings might be unsurprising. Turning away from intentional self-disclosure, Wosket (1999: 11) explains that:

> Therapists inadvertently reveal themselves in innumerable small ways as they present themselves to clients through such aspects as dress, accent, age, voice intonation, skin colour, involuntary changes in movement or facial expression, mannerisms, the furnishings and state of orderliness of the counselling room, and so on.

Of course, our clients will pick up on unspoken clues as we all do in everyday life. We are not talking of secrecy here, which hints at control, but rather of discretion, and the practice of well-considered and helpful sharing that contributes to the therapeutic relationship.

WORKING ETHICALLY WITH SURVIVORS OF SEXUAL ABUSE

When working with clients who have a history of sexual abuse, we are required to increase our awareness of our sexual boundaries, including touch, our use of language and the level of our closeness. We should be careful not to make our client uncomfortable by using any physical or verbal communication that might be misconstrued. Many counsellors have a policy of not touching any client for that very reason. Survivors of sexual abuse respond in different ways during counselling as there are an infinite number of factors that can influence their level of engagement. As such, we should remain alert to these being communicated to us. Another influencing factor might be when our client experienced their abuse as childhood sexual abuse who may respond differently to adult survivors. They may find it particularly difficult to establish and maintain relationships and the element of trust may be additionally challenging. The disempowerment that is associated with non-consensual sexual violence can have long-lasting consequences. A client who has survived such an experience may experience reoccurring symptoms; fear, persistent memories, post-traumatic stress disorder (PTSD), numbing, addiction issues, psychological distress, depression and suicidal ideation. Adult survivors can also develop a range of coping strategies, some of which might be unhealthy. Working therapeutically with any of these issues can introduce an additional perspective which can be helpful to discuss with our client. Any conscious or unconscious overstepping of appropriate limits risks exacerbating our client's condition, reinforcing underlying trust beliefs and rupturing our alliance.

A FRAMEWORK OF WORKING WITH SEXUAL ISSUES WITHIN SAFE, APPROPRIATE AND CLEAR BOUNDARIES

It can be considerably easier to establish clear guidelines when we are not actually in a situation that requires evaluation of our sexual boundaries. If we are able to take a strategic approach and establish a framework should we find ourselves in that position, it can reduce an element of stress by reminding us of our limits when influenced by the current relationship. The following five statements are taken from professional bodies that guide the therapeutic landscape:

COSCA Statement of Ethics *(2014)*

> 7.2 A member must not exploit a client, financially, emotionally, sexually or in any other way which does not give attention primarily to the best interests of the client.

BPS Code of Ethics and Conduct *(2009)*

> 4.3 Standard of maintaining personal boundaries (i) Refrain from engaging in any form of sexual or romantic relationship with persons to whom they are providing professional services, or to whom they owe a continuing duty of care, or with whom they have a relationship of trust. This might include a former patient, a student or trainee, or a junior staff member.

BABCP Standards of Conduct, Performance and Ethics *(2010)*

1. You must act in the best interests of service users

1.1 You are personally responsible for making sure that you promote and protect the best interests of your service users. You must respect and take account of these factors when providing care or a service, and must not abuse the relationship you have with a service user, sexually, emotionally, financially or in other ways.

BACP Ethical Framework for the Counselling Professions *(2015)*

34. We will not have sexual relationships with or behave sexually towards our clients, supervisees or trainees.

35. We will avoid having sexual relationships with or behaving sexually towards people whom we know to be close to our clients in order to avoid undermining our clients' trust in us.

36. We will not exploit or abuse our clients in any way: financially, emotionally, physically, sexually or spiritually.

UKCP Ethical Principles and Code of Professional Conduct *(2009)*

1.3 The psychotherapist undertakes not to abuse or exploit the relationship they have with their clients, current or past, for any purpose, including the psychotherapist's sexual, emotional or financial gain.

1.4 The psychotherapist undertakes not to enter into a sexual relationship with a client.

We can see from these a very clear line to take: act in the client's best interest; remain within the role of professional; do not exploit or take advantage of the client in any way and do not have sexual relationships with clients.

AREAS FOR CONCERN AND POTENTIAL CHALLENGES

This can be a challenging area to address for some counsellors. Rather than discuss possible areas for concern here, it may be more helpful to identify your own. This will depend upon your confidence and comfort discussing challenging and sometimes embarrassing situations, your approach to acknowledging spoken and unspoken communication within the counselling room and your ability to bring any suspicions or aspects of concern into the therapeutic process.

Questions for reflection

1. What do I understand by sexual boundaries?
2. How do I manage my own behaviours, thoughts and feelings?
3. What level of self-disclosure am I comfortable with?
4. Might my own personal history impact on my comfort level addressing this subject?
5. How comfortable do I feel addressing sexual issues in an open manner?

FURTHER READING

Celenza, A. (2011). *Sexual boundary violations: therapeutic, supervisory, and academic contexts.* Plymouth, MA: Jason Aronson.

Doré, P., & Williamson, A. (2016). *Unsafe spaces: why the lack of regulation in counselling and psychotherapy is endangering vulnerable people.* Available at: www.unsafespaces.com

Martin, C., Godfrey, M., Meekums, B., & Madill, A. (2011). Managing boundaries under pressure: a qualitative study of therapists' experiences of sexual attraction in therapy. *Counselling and Psychotherapy Research, 11*(4), 248–256.

Norris, D.M., Gutheil, T.G., & Strasburger, L.H. (2003). This couldn't happen to me: boundary problems and sexual misconduct in the psychotherapy relationship. *Psychiatric Services, 54*(4), 517–522.

7

SAYING GOODBYE: THERAPEUTIC AND ETHICAL ENDINGS

This chapter will focus on how we can maintain a safe and ethical relationship during the final stage of the therapeutic process. We'll consider the number of different ways in which therapy can end: sometimes problematic, other times therapeutic. There are several ways in which counsellors can maximise the therapeutic potential of working with endings which we will consider. Our clinical supervision can play a key role in supporting us during times of concern.

BEGINNINGS AND ENDINGS

In most counselling training, the terms beginning, middle and ending are well used to delineate stages in the therapeutic process. Out of habit, we often concentrate on the meaning and context of these stages rather than the words themselves and more precisely, how they may be interpreted by clients. 'Beginnings' suggests the start of something new; it might involve excitement, trepidation, aspects of development and on the whole, tends to be viewed in a positive light. So far, we have discussed beginnings at length in respect to contracting, negotiating, explaining and introducing. Middles and endings have been slightly less represented. It is well accepted that the middle stages of the therapeutic process relate to the use of the counselling skills relevant to the counsellor's theoretical orientation and are the filling in the counselling sandwich. How many sessions make up this stage depends upon the initial agreed number of meetings. Endings however, can be less predictable and often viewed less positively. This can depend upon the issues the client shared, their level of confidence and their sense of progress or completion. Time spent bringing the therapeutic relationship to a close can also be unpredictable, so our sensitivity to each individual relationship will indicate what is, and is not, appropriate. One immediate consideration is our phraseology. In contexts other than counselling, we use many words to mean ending and our choice of vocabulary can have a significant impact on how ourselves and our clients view this final stage. Our own approach to ending the counselling is particularly pertinent when working with a client who has shared difficulties involving change or loss in the context of relationships.

Read through the following list of terminology and reflect on any feeling each word triggers in you. Consider which might be heard as positive or negative:

- finish
- closure
- conclusion
- culmination
- resolution
- summing up
- denouement
- finale
- cessation
- stop
- termination.

You may have found that you were more comfortable with some words than others. This may well be the same for clients and a high level of sensitivity is required. For example, an obvious consideration would be if working with a client who had shared their unhappiness following an abortion, it would be less appropriate to talk of terminating the counselling. Some terms sound more positive, such as culmination, resolution and summing up. These intrinsically suggest a positive outcome, whereas cessation, stop and termination are rather more stern. It may sound obvious, but we need to reflect on and work with the terminology that is most fitting for each individual client.

How long we have known our client can also have an impact on the manner in which we approach the ending of therapy. With short term work, we can't assume that there is any less depth achieved in the process or relational bond than in long term work. The main difference is that there may be considerably less time available to focus on closure. If we only have six weeks together, it is possible that only the final session can be allocated for closure. Alternatively, if we are always working towards our client being an independent, autonomous person, we might touch on aspects of ending at some point within each session. Longer term work allows for greater time dedicated to the rounding up of the issues and the relationship.

DIFFERENT WAYS IN WHICH THERAPY CAN END

As just mentioned, unlike many other professional relationships, the therapeutic relationship begins with both counsellor and client looking at reaching a point in the future where the relationship will finish. Even if a client is attending for self-reflection and self-development, there will still be a point whereby it would be difficult to justify the continuation of the relationship. Depending upon the setting in which the service is based, there might be a more expected or predicted ending. There is already much literature identifying and exploring endings that are either planned and unplanned. However, it is helpful to consider the end of therapy not as a single final session but rather as a drawing to a close of a process which can take a number of sessions. If a client has been working through a number of issues it may be efficacious to focus on closure for each issue, individually, which can take time. This is a favoured method within a number of modalities and is designed to leave the client with a very clear sense of progress, self-management and closure. Alternatively, viewing the issues more holistically can result in greater cohesiveness which reinforces the connections and links that have been considered during the therapy. The client may then leave with a heightened sense of their life as a whole, rather than a group of segments.

ENDINGS AS PROBLEMATIC

Finishing with a client isn't always straightforward and can be problematic for the client, the counsellor, or both. There are many ways in which the final stage of therapy can raise challenges for both client and counsellor. Read the following example and identify which issues might be unhelpful for the client's progress.

Juliette was referred for counselling through her employer's Occupational Health department after attending a health assessment session where she shared that she was feeling very low following the breakdown of her marriage. She wasn't referred for a total number of sessions but the counsellor was asked to provide ongoing evaluation and finally Juliette was funded to attend 20 sessions. During their time together, she seemed to view the sessions as a time to tell stories about her life but avoided any mention of feelings. When challenged, she admitted that she felt the need to 'put on a face' with everyone in her life, particularly at work where she was known as the life and soul of the party.

It became clear to the counsellor that Juliette's skill at appearing happy extended into the therapy room and that she had a conscious awareness of her avoidance to engage with any deeper reflection. When invited to attend an occupational health assessment she used her well-practised persona of the joker and her OH staff felt that, despite it being an act, she demonstrated an ability to perform successfully at work. Funding was subsequently withdrawn.

This situation was particularly problematic for a number of reasons, which include:

- There was no set agreement regarding the number of sessions at the outset.
- Parallel assessment was carried out by both the counsellor and the funder which didn't concur.
- It wasn't her idea. Juliette attended counselling out of fear of losing her job if she didn't.
- Had she decided to continue, the client couldn't afford to pay for additional sessions.
- Juliette had very little control or power in this situation.
- Despite her false affect being recognised as a coping strategy as opposed to an improvement, it was cheaper to assess it as sufficient and withdraw ongoing support.

This ending would have been more beneficial and professional if any of the following had been addressed:

- The client and the counsellor had an idea of the available funding at the outset and therefore the number of sessions available.
- The definition of progress was judged externally and linked to the ability to function at work rather than the client's own therapeutic progress.

- The employer had recognised that a therapeutic assessment and an evaluation of ability to work are two very different processes.
- The client had been actively involved in the decision-making process and it had been explained that attending counselling was not punitive and not linked to job security.
- The client felt totally reliant on her employer as she was unable to afford continuing or alternative therapy.
- The client and the OH department agreed an aim or purpose to the therapy prior to the first session.

If our client is attending counselling with issues relating to loss or abandonment, resistance to change or lack of connectedness, ending the counselling relationship, however well planned, can be challenging. It is important that the ending is viewed as successful closure and, depending upon the modality of therapy used, is an opportunity to put a newly realised reality or learned coping strategies into place.

Another example would be when an ending is out of the hands of client and counsellor, such as in an educational setting where counselling is only available for registered students. It can be very hard when a student completes their course but is right in the middle of working through their ongoing issues. In this case referral might be frustrating but necessary. The other side of this coin is that both client and counsellor should know when the course ends and use that date as a final session, thereby building towards a planned ending. If a student is asked to leave their course mid-term, it can be considerably more challenging.

Consider this situation:

Felicity is in her second year of an art degree. She is attending counselling as she was sexually assaulted last year and it has had a very detrimental effect on all aspects of her life. She finds it very difficult to concentrate and has subsequently fallen behind on all her assessments. The university have told her that she is so far behind that she can no longer attend the course.

Here we can see that Felicity's situation is a direct result of the assault and as such, the therapeutic work taking place whilst attending the student counselling service would be a key way to support her to re-engage with her course. The challenges for the counsellor here are numerous and might include:

1. a lack of control
2. a sense of failure
3. Felicity's fears or disappointment
4. frustration at a lack of care by the organisation
5. a sudden break in the therapeutic alliance reinforcing any undermining of trust issues
6. the introduction of stresses surrounding referral.

This scenario might be particularly problematic because of the external locus of control that has resulted in neither Felicity or her counsellor making a decision regarding their ending.

ENDINGS AS THERAPEUTIC

We know that our work with our clients is an alliance. If we are used to working within an agreed time limit, we will become experienced in managing planned endings. The efficacy of the counselling process can be richly enhanced by a well planned and clearly structured ending. Integrating the concept of the future into the counselling process ensures that the ending of the therapy sessions marks the beginning of a new phase for our client. If we are promoting independence and self-sufficiency, then the consideration of past, present and future should be providing the overarching structure to our work. It would be unrealistic and unhelpful to position ourselves within any of the stages other than 'present', so our client should be encouraged to consider their future with their new insights, ability to reframe situations and successful coping strategies.

This was demonstrated by Jean. During her third session she had a 'lightbulb moment' that brought clarity to a situation which had previously been causing her frustration and confusion. She was able to view her reactions and take time to consider how she might integrate this new awareness in her future. This allowed her three further sessions to work through her new understanding but also, to decide for herself when her final session should be. She was very clear about when she felt attending counselling was no longer needed.

Unlike with Jean, the unplanned ending of a client simply never returning or replying to further contact can be both puzzling and challenging. Puzzling in that during the time we have worked together, whether short or long term, we have come to care about our client as an individual. We may have unanswered questions and may never know why they stopped attending. It is a natural reaction to jump to the conclusion that the counselling wasn't meeting their needs and start to doubt ourselves in terms of our skill, ability and observation. Why didn't we notice that they weren't happy or comfortable? However, whilst non-attendance without any communication might be impolite, it is not automatically a negative outcome.

> Leanne made an appointment to see the school counsellor. After discussing and agreeing to a six-week contract, she spent the rest of the first session talking about her recent argument with her boyfriend who was in the same class. She was clearly upset and thought they had split up. When she didn't attend her second session the counsellor emailed her to check that she was alright and to offer her the opportunity to schedule a second appointment. Leanne replied with a very short email stating that the counselling had 'worked', she was back with her boyfriend and that she didn't need any more appointments.

This scenario is typical of the different mindsets that client and counsellor can have with regard to commitment, purpose and depth of the counselling meetings. Despite Leanne taking an equal and active role in the initial contracting, and the counsellor feeling she had an understanding of the process, the client had a single reason for attending, whereas the counsellor viewed the bigger picture. This example highlights the potential differences in both reasons for attending but, more importantly, how a client might view a successful outcome compared to a counsellor's idea of a successful outcome. Leanne was focusing on the current situation – the here and now – whereas the counsellor might well have been considering the past and future as well. However, the following week a new client started who told the counsellor that Leanne had recommended she make an appointment as the counselling was *really good and really helped her*.

WAYS IN WHICH COUNSELLORS CAN MAXIMISE THE THERAPEUTIC POTENTIAL OF WORKING WITH ENDINGS

There are numerous methods for using the ending process to build on the alliance that has developed throughout the time of working together. For example, encouraging the client to conduct their own evaluation and assessment allows them to identify aspects of development that the counsellor might not be fully aware of. Using session notes to form a comparison between the first week and the current week is also a useful way of helping a client to measure their journey. The use of outcome measures also illustrate change in a more formal way. It is also helpful to spend time with the client looking at how they may approach possible future challenges and how they can implement any new ways of thinking. Ideally, the acknowledgment that the client today is not who they were when they first entered the counselling room can provide a confidence and trust in their current self which is a significant step. This is a situation that often arises when working with changed behaviours such as phobias, addictions or dependency issues. Clients commonly express a fear of future tests to their resolve as they are associating with their old behaviours and attitudes and not fully trusting their new ones. Identifying this lack of acceptance and unconscious resistance means it can be integrated into the process of closure, so the client is leaving with a sense of strength and growth. This strength and growth can be used as a measure for ourselves too as evidence of our ability to successfully facilitate psychological development.

ROLE OF CLINICAL SUPERVISION

It is not just our client who may have fears or be struggling with the concept of moving on. We too can experience a sense of loss or resistance to the therapy ending. Having worked closely with a client we genuinely like, it would be unrealistic not to expect to miss contact with them and to wonder occasionally how they are doing. It can be difficult to have confidence in our client and their future if we don't have confidence in ourself and our ability to promote and support development.

This can be gained and built on using regular reflection, monitoring, learning and questioning of what we do and how we do it. Thus, the ending of the therapeutic alliance can be reframed to become the start of the next phase for the client and the next phase for us. When working in supervision, the ending and completion of work with a particular client can be used to identify and reinforce positive work and identify and explore aspects that were less successful.

LEAVING THE DOOR OPEN FOR THE FUTURE

The concept of working with the same client in the future might be unrealistic if we are working within a large organisation or a statutory service. If it is a possibility, it can be reassuring for our client to know that if a situation should arise in the future and they wish to return to counselling, they are able to meet with the same counsellor. By this I don't mean in a dependent way, but rather in a progressive way. The client wouldn't have to start at the beginning and retell their history, but would be able to continue with a counsellor who already knew them. They would be able to refer to situations and examples that had already arisen in previous sessions and they would have a trusting relationship in place for the first session.

AREAS FOR CONCERN AND POTENTIAL CHALLENGES

The topic of dependency can often raise its head when considering the ending of a counselling relationship. Dependency isn't always a negative: Amis (2008: 181) claims that '*In some approaches dependency is viewed as helpful and is positively encouraged*' – but in this current context it can be. Reliance on the counselling meetings or the relationship with the counsellor can raise issues of loss, change and closure, developing a culture of dependence rather than independence.

When encouraging the client to identify change, remember to integrate and implement their new coping strategies. A previous client admitted that when in a difficult spot would ask himself, 'What would Kirsten say?', which was simply his technique for accessing the content of our sessions. This very quickly evolved into 'What do I know that I should do here?' and, finally 'What did I do last time this happened?', which is a healthy and positive technique to make conscious decisions. Referring to his counsellor was simply a temporary tool that prompted a new and more positive way of thinking.

The counsellor/client relationship may be considered to extend beyond the arranged sessions, not with regard to therapy but in terms of the nature of the relationship. If your client saw you three months after the final session, they would still think of you in terms of being their ex-counsellor. This is acknowledged within professional standards. The BPS (2009) state in section 4.2 '*(v) Recognise that conflicts of interests and inequity of power may still reside after professional relationships are formally terminated, such that professional responsibilities may still apply.*' This is referring to our ongoing responsibility to act in an ethical and professional manner if any contact is maintained. The BACP also acknowledge the implications of a past professional relationship in section 37:

> We recognise that conflicts of interest and issues of power or dependence may continue after our working relationship with a client, supervisee or trainee has formally ended. We will exercise caution before entering into personal or business relationships with former clients and expect to be professionally accountable if the relationship becomes detrimental to the former client or the standing of the profession. (BACP, 2015: 9)

In practice, this means that the ending of our therapeutic alliance is not the end of our professional responsibilities. We still have a duty to behave appropriately and in keeping with our original contract if we are to see an ex-client in the future.

Questions for reflection

1. What do endings mean to me?
2. What aspects of endings do I find most challenging?
3. How do I keep alert to unhelpful dependency issues?
4. What might I do to Improve my management of endings?
5. How do I process my own loss when a client moves on?

FURTHER READING

Leigh, A. (1998). *Referral and termination issues for counsellors.* London: Sage.

Murdin, L. (2000). *How much is enough? Endings in psychotherapy and counselling.* London: Routledge.

Robson, M. (2008a). Working with a planned ending. In W. Dryden, & A. Reeves (eds), *Key issues for counselling in action.* London: Sage.

Robson, M. (2008b). Anticipating and working with unplanned endings. In W. Dryden, & A. Reeves (eds), *Key issues for counselling in action.* London: Sage.

8

REPAIRING RUPTURES AND ATTENDING TO DIFFICULTIES

Working successfully and remaining confident with ruptures, challenges and complaints can sometimes feel overwhelming or beyond our reach. This chapter focuses on some commonly experienced challenges and suggests how we might respond in a professional, non-defensive way, integrating the issues into our therapy. It encourages developing the ability to separate our professional responsibilities from our personal world, so we don't automatically hear challenge as a personal attack. To accept challenge as an additional form of communication leads to us including it within the therapeutic process.

CHANGES AND DISRUPTIONS TO BOUNDARIES THAT ARISE AS PART OF EVERYDAY PRACTICE

Very new counselling relationships may initially progress without any sort of disruption or change as the counsellor and client are learning whether their newly agreed contract meets their needs. However, once the counselling alliance develops, it could be argued that without change, the relationship and process may become too stagnant to remain therapeutic. Change may well make us uncomfortable at the time but it is our ability to successfully evolve and adapt to change that indicates how robust we are as therapists.

We know that conflicting values, principles and responsibilities precipitate any boundary challenge which we should explore before making a decision. A knee-jerk reaction is often detrimental to the therapeutic process following such a challenge. However, in addition to settings where we may be in a position to make change, there are also times that highlight potentially unethical situations in which we may feel powerless. These might include:

1. a new, inexperienced trainee working with vulnerable clients for the first time to gain experience managing risk
2. a trainee finding themselves in a placement with very little support
3. a trainee may be expected to work with a supervisor provided by the course which introduces an ethical conflict if they are also in the role of lecturers or tutor
4. a counsellor required to accept supervision from a colleague who is also their line manager.

In all these situations, the trainee or counsellor may feel that they are conflicted as the boundaries are being externally set and do not meet their personal or professional ethical framework.

Consider the following situation we have all been through which highlights how challenging it can be to respond when feeling that a boundary is under pressure:

> For the sake of transparency and to facilitate informed decision making, when we are gaining experience on placement, we are told it is compulsory to inform our clients that we are currently in training.
>
> • Is a simple disclosure of lack of experience sufficient to safeguard the wellbeing of the client?
> • Might a client feel too embarrassed or uncomfortable to ask for a more experienced counsellor?
> • What else might we consider?

The manner in which we identify a need for change or present it to our client will have a significant impact on their confidence to be honest. It might be straightforward to tell a client that we care for them but when boundaries are under pressure it says more if we are able to demonstrate that we do. This is when we need to find an appropriate balance between doing something above and beyond what might be expected whilst still working within our professional boundaries and remaining ethically robust. For example, sending a text message asking after a client who has missed a session might be well received. It can be difficult to work out what the right thing to do at that time is so that we manage the fine line between professional (sometimes felt as distant) and personal (overly familiar). It's difficult enough to consider it in a 'what if' situation, but considerably more challenging at the time when under pressure with someone you have got to know. At this point it is helpful to revert to Bond's steps of ethical decision making, especially the step that asks 'Consider who holds responsibility for resolving the problem' (Bond, 2010: 227–238).

EXAMPLES OF DISRUPTIONS AND CHALLENGES

Disruption and challenge can also arise when there is a position of risk. It is our responsibility to assess any perceived or actual risk and make an informed decision as a result of that assessment. Again, if we have already developed and agreed a clear, therapeutic contract, we can work through the situation together and agree a way of working with the risk. Consider this scenario:

> During Donald's eighth session, he discloses that he is planning how to take his life. He shares his plans with you.

What do you do now that both your safety and confidentiality boundaries are under pressure? This example was left intentionally vague so that you can see how important it is to gather as much information as possible; not in a pressured or interrogatory manner but from a position of care. To make an informed decision, we require as much information as possible.

Consider your basic safety checklist:

- What does the client want you to do with this information?
- What does the law say you should do?
- What do our ethical guidelines tell us to do?
- What is the organisation's policy or procedure in this situation?

You might notice that these considerations don't just involve reflection but lead to some form of action. Now consider a different situation which may also be challenging for some:

> You are the only counsellor working in the local GP surgery. Ismat attends her first session and brings her sister with her who she insists also comes into the counselling session. She says that it's because you are male and she needs to have a chaperone with her or her husband wouldn't let her attend.

This situation touches on several challenges to our usual way of working in a one-to-one session including cultural norms and expectations, perception of personal safety and confidentiality issues. There is also the additional influence of another person who is not present. What would you take into consideration during the contracting process?

- Is Ismat sufficiently comfortable with the arrangement so that it adds to rather than detracts from the counselling?
- Any influence that the sister's presence might have on the therapeutic content.
- Is gender going to have a negative impact on the counselling?
- Are you aware how the presence of Ismat's sister will consciously or unconsciously influence the content of the sessions?
- Is there any way to access a female counsellor if it were Ismat's preference?
- What other influence might Ismat's husband have on her?

It is perfectly possible to find a workable solution to this situation in which all four parties are happy, but to do so will include considering alternative ways of working that might differ from our usual set-up. Ensuring that we put our client first and maintain a safe environment can include a range of ways of working that may involve some lateral thinking, collaboration with our client and reflection with our supervisor; our responsibility to provide an equitable service might take us out of our comfort zone. The main factor is to consider the situation from the client's perspective and not to stretch our working practices to the point where they become unsafe or are unjustifiable.

TENSION THAT ARISES BETWEEN CHOOSING TO HOLD BOUNDARIES FIRMLY OR RESPONDING TO CLIENT'S FLEXIBILITY

How we manage our sessions can be challenging but as long as we are constantly evaluating and assessing the client within the context of their development, we should be on the right track. It depends very much on which boundary is under pressure and why.

As discussed in Chapter 1, there are boundaries that are agreed within the relationship and those that are predetermined by external factors. The former tend to be significantly more flexible than the latter. We are unlikely to be able to change boundaries that are dictated by law, ethical guidelines and organisational policies and procedures as they are usually the result of a professional consultation process and intended to maintain rigorous standards of practice and safety for those involved. If you don't agree with a particular guideline, it is always possible to pass on your objection to the authoring committee with the reasons why, but that doesn't mean that we don't have to adhere to them.

Working with the flexible boundaries is a far more autonomous process but the cause of the tension becomes more relevant. We know that the client/counsellor contract for therapy is a working document and as such should be open for regular review. If the client is made aware at the outset which aspects are flexible and which are not, the process becomes far easier.

> Wayne is moving house. He estimates that it will take him three hours to drive to his sessions from his new house. He is asking what the alternatives are.

Revisiting the contents of the contract from Chapter 3 will offer some structure to assessing any possible flexibility.

First, ascertain exactly which boundary is under tension. Then use clear questions to clarify the query in relation to yourself and your client. Finally, discuss possible courses of action with the client being clear to explain why any choices might not be an option. The following reflective questions might appear obvious but are important to help establish if we are over-personalising any challenge and feeling a tension when maybe the client isn't.

- Assessment – Is it the initial or the ongoing assessment that is being challenged? What is the actual request? What is the client's suggested solution? For example, Sharon asks if she can see her initial assessment to see if she agrees with it.
- Beginnings and endings – Is the client challenging the timing, progress or length of the process? For example, Barbara doesn't feel that eight sessions are sufficient and asks for additional sessions.
- Competence – How confident do you feel in managing the tension? Would you benefit from support? Is the client challenging your competence or are you doubting your own competence? What is the evidence this is based on? For example, Dominic says to you '*I don't know if this is working or not. You don't seem to be doing very much*'.
- Complaints procedure – Do they have a copy? Is it clearly available? Are they wishing to complain? Is it about you, the service or more general? Does the client feel supported in this?
- Confidentiality – Are they questioning how confidential the session content is? Are they asking you to break confidentiality? Have they shared the session content with others? Are they unhappy with the confidentiality limits they agreed to during the initial contracting? For example, Catherine tells you that she discusses her sessions each week with her friend.

- Contracts – Are they wanting to revisit, renegotiate or terminate the initial contract? Do they wish to draw up a new contract?
- Dual relationships – What is the nature of the secondary relationship? Is it temporary or permanent? Is it ethical?
- Missing/rescheduling a session – Have they kept you informed of any absence or just not turned up? Are they asking for a new time that is possible to accommodate? For example, Jim tells you that he is unable to attend on a Thursday any more as his shifts at work have changed. He is asking for his appointments to be moved to a different day.
- Monitoring and evaluation through reflective practice (this links to assessment) – How involved is the client in the process? Are they aware of what takes place and why? Are they involved in any changes that result from ongoing evaluation? What is their preferred solution?
- Number of sessions – Is this fixed or flexible? Who is funding the sessions and is additional funding available? Are you restricted by a waiting list? Are there dependency issues? Is the change justified?
- Record keeping – Is the client challenging why, how or what is recorded? Is their query linked to confidentiality? Are they asking for access to or copies of their notes? What is your policy regarding access to notes?
- Referral – What are they actually requesting and why? Is referral possible? Is the request personal, professional or external? What does it mean to you?
- Roles – Are they asking you to clarify what they do? Do you feel it's in a questioning, critical or constructive way? Why might this have arisen?
- Settings – What is the exact challenge? Are they wishing to challenge the service? Is funding involved? For example, Fiona was made redundant last week. She is no longer able to afford the hourly rate for her sessions. She asks if she can get a referral via her GP.
- Storing notes – This tends to be one of the least flexible aspects. Are they asking where notes are stored or how secure they are? Are they wanting to know for how long or who has access to them?
- Supervision – Is the question about who the supervisor is or more generally about the relationship. Are they asking what is discussed or how you are monitored?
- Theoretical orientation – Is your underpinning theory being questioned or your practice/use of skills? Is the client considering alternative options? Are they saying that the methodology being used is or isn't working for them? Are they disagreeing with any aspects? What would they prefer?
- Timing of sessions – Are sessions too long, too short, too often or not often enough? What would they rather and why? Is that reasonable, possible or justified?
- Training and experience – Are they questioning your qualifications, asking where or when you trained? Is this from interest or is it linked to questioning your competence?

COUNSELLOR-LED RUPTURES

Personal blocks and difficulties that therapists face that
can weaken their ability to work in this way

Although the establishment of boundaries reassures many counsellors and clients, it can also frustrate others. Working within guidelines suits those of us who like a clear structure: the list makers of the world. There are those of us however, who find them stifling and restrictive. If a counsellor or client prefers a more organic, creative or spontaneous way of working it can be challenging to find a method of defining the boundaries that allows for a freer way of working. Being able to reframe contracting so that it strengthens and reinforces the therapeutic work whilst still maintaining safety is a skill that develops over time and in itself can require a fair amount of creativity! To illustrate this, imagine working in a counselling service within a school. You have a new client who is restless and uncommunicative and you feel that the environment that you are in isn't conducive to your client trusting you. You feel that the right thing to do would be to suggest to the client that you both go for a walk as it would feel less formal and would ease the pressure, such as for eye contact. Unfortunately, the school doesn't support taking pupils out during the day without completing a risk assessment, getting signed permission from the parent or guardian and entering it into the school diary in advance. This is a situation whereby the externally enforced boundaries may well be impeding the therapeutic process. There is no argument that they are clearly there for the safety of both pupil and adult but not necessarily helpful for client and counsellor. This can lead to frustration for the counsellor who has to then find an ethical and legal way to work with this barrier to enable a less rigid approach in the future. It also reduces all spontaneity from a more creative way of meeting the needs of different clients and is an example of both client and counsellor being disempowered. If you were in this situation, what would you do?

Hopefully you considered:

- asking your client if there was somewhere else in the school that they would rather sit
- issues of confidentiality and how your client might feel if they were seen with you
- making your counselling environment less daunting to clients
- formulating a plan for accommodating this situation should it occur again in the future

- feeding back to your line manager in the school the helpful and unhelpful aspects of the policies and procedures in the context of counselling.

Another personal block might be a lack of confidence or experience in your management of the process. It is more straightforward when we are provided with a contract that is a rigid set of rules that can't be altered. It comes with its own challenges but at least it is clear cut. When a professional is afforded an element of flexibility and personal autonomy, some can find it daunting. To illustrate this, just consider working with a client at risk. If this situation is new, we have no previous experience to refer back to or learn from. We are responsible for making decisions and choices that can directly impact on the life and safety of another. On one hand it would be easy and superficially helpful to have a clear list of instructions to follow, whether that be from the organisation, our lead body's ethical framework, the law or our supervisor. On the other, that would detract from the uniqueness of each individual client and their personal circumstances and feelings by assuming our clients' situations are the same as each other. By being given broad guidelines with elements of freedom, we are being trusted as professional practitioners who have the ability to work with our client to find the right path for them. Some counsellors see this as an appropriate freedom that values them and their abilities whilst others find it frustrating and woolly. It is helpful to take any negative feelings to supervision for further exploration. If we are expecting our client to test new ground, develop coping strategies and feel empowered, why aren't we comfortable with finding ourselves in a similar situation? We have a responsibility to our clients, ourselves and our profession to develop a safe way of working that embodies this ethos. As long as we have successfully passed our training and demonstrated that we are fit and safe to practise, we should trust ourselves and justify our decision making.

   It is quite common for newly practising counsellors to unfairly assume a disproportionate amount of responsibility for the therapeutic process in a counselling session when progress isn't going to a speed the counsellor expects. They may blame themselves rather than considering the role and responsibility of the client in the process. We may spend only 50 minutes out of a possible 10,080 minutes a week with the client and yet we can easily fall into the trap of assuming that our session has more power over the life of the client than it actually does. Although hopefully, we are aware of what takes place when the client is sitting with us and assume that the client is open and honest with regard to their thought processes. However, once a client leaves the room, thoughts don't immediately stop. The therapeutic process can continue and we have no idea how the client is organising their thoughts. Therefore, it seems illogical and unfair to blame ourselves if the client does not appear to be progressing at an arbitrary rate that we might expect them to. A fairer approach would surely be to involve the client in a regular evaluation process whereby any progress (or not) can be identified by the client themselves. This demonstrates a more equitable method based on the client's own viewpoint. It also offers the counsellor opportunity to reflect on their role in supporting and encouraging the client throughout the therapeutic relationship.

FEE NEGOTIATIONS

The issue of funding can, for some, provide a difficulty if our client isn't always in control of the payment for their sessions. While statutory settings are paid indirectly via National Insurance Contributions, clients often have to abide by the decision of a budget holder such as their GP. In voluntary settings there is greater leeway for negotiation as many voluntary counselling services do not have an hourly charge for sessions but offer clients the opportunity to make an affordable donation. More commonly, they are funded by a combination of fundraising and successful tendering processes, so a percentage of their funding may well derive from the statutory sector too.

It is when clients attend counselling in a private setting that fee negotiations are more likely. Many counsellors are quite uncomfortable discussing money with their clients. It helps to consider how we might feel no embarrassment when discussing the cost of a service with a hairdresser, car mechanic or plumber, yet we are seen by our clients in the same way. Being open and including an honest discussion on cost during contracting will increase the likelihood of clients telling us if their financial situation has changed. The following should also be developed:

- Do you charge a client who misses a session?
- Do you charge a client who cancels a session?
- Do you charge a client who is struggling financially?

Fees may be determined by the organisation or the individual counsellor and it is in this situation that unplanned breaks may occur if a client's financial situation deteriorates. In some cultures, bartering is a perfectly accepted method of exchanging services (see discussion within Chapter 5) but this can introduce additional pressure to managing safe and appropriate boundaries so is not encouraged. A typical scaling might look like this:

One session	£45
Six sessions	£250
Twelve sessions	£450
Concessionary rate (student, job seeker, low/no wage)	£negotiable
Cancelled with less than 24 hrs notice	£25

The fees will depend upon the location of the service and can differ significantly across the country. Being in private practice can be expensive to manage, especially if working from home. There are strict health and safety and professional environmental factors to consider, such as having different doors for family and clients, access to a private toilet, sufficiently distant from natural noise from your family, etc. The cost of alterations can be expensive making it more challenging for some counsellors to be able to offer a reduced rate. Continuity can be maintained if alternative funding can be accessed, e.g. a private client accessing continuing funding from their GP.

CHANGES TO THE SETTING/ENVIRONMENT

Other disruptions that can be experienced include changes to our counselling environment. From experience, being based within a large organisation can result in a compulsory, unplanned move within the premises, or to another building entirely. This can be poorly received by clients, particularly those who rely on the predictability and learned safety of sessions in the original environment.

Working in a rural area may bring additional considerations. Depending upon the nature of the disruption, there may be few alternatives for a client due to the lack of available or alternative counselling services. If referral isn't an option, creative solutions may have to be found to facilitate the continuation of our client attending. Of course, any solution must remain ethical and appropriate, but by placing the needs of the client first, working within their consent and ensuring a safe transition, there should be minimal disruption to the therapeutic alliance.

CHALLENGES TO THE BOUNDARIES THAT MAY COME FROM THE THERAPIST

Additional challenges may be introduced as we further develop our ways of working therapeutically. Many current changes to practice are more developmental as a result of technological and research developments. These might include the introduction of 'Walk and Talk' sessions, the option of VOIP services (such as Skype) and additional training in online therapies. Clearly we are unlikely to change our method of therapy during an ongoing relationship, but having the skills and the opportunity to offer these as an alternative, might meet the needs of some clients. It is crucial that the counsellor is confident and suitably trained in any alternative method so there is no rupture in the therapeutic process. It also ensures that there is not a situation where the new method is more challenging for the counsellor than for the client. This raises the question: 'Are we embedded in traditional practice to the exclusion of potentially new and successful methodologies?' or are we open to flexibility so that our practice meets the needs of our clients? There are a number of factors to consider here such as the age and preferences of our client, their likelihood to maintain regular attendance (e.g. students only being home during holidays), the physical ability of the client, their ability and comfort with the agreed method and the network and equipment necessary to facilitate it. It is not helpful or professional for our inability to master the method of therapy to then detract from the therapy itself.

In addition to this, there is our ethical responsibility for our own self-care. We should be in the habit of acknowledging and acting on an awareness of when we should not be working. This might be due to our personal circumstances and we should regulate our working responsibilities to reflect this. As counsellors, we are not infallible and there are significant additional pressures if we are self-employed or financially vulnerable. Establishing a strategy for managing any period when it would not be safe for us to practise should be paramount.

COUNSELLOR'S SELF-DISCLOSURE

Another area that can cause a rupture in our alliance is the level to which we share information about ourselves. We have already considered self-disclosure in the context of sexual boundaries (Chapter 6) but sharing our experiences is a sensitive intervention and one that can raise many issues, one of which is a rupture to our relationship with our client. We may know we are constantly disclosing coded information such as in the clothes we wear, the way we speak, our accent and the way we choose to present our therapy room, which our clients can interpret, but the decision to give more overt, described information about ourselves is a very personal and thorny issue. Commonly used in addiction services, the sharing of personal history and experiences is often used as a therapeutic tool; 'I may appear to be the expert but actually if I can do it then so can you', 'I am talking from a position of personal knowledge and previous experience', etc. It is crucial to reflect on why we feel the need to pass on information and who it will benefit. Remember that any information offered can't then be retracted if later we regret it. The following questions can be used as a framework to reflect on your own limits and comfort around self-disclosure:

- Am I motivated by my own desire to share to become closer or more understood by my client?
- How is it relevant or beneficial to what is happening in the therapeutic process?
- What reaction am I expecting?
- Why do I want my client to know that aspect of myself?
- What might the impact be on our relationship?
- Will this disclosure overstep any professional or personal boundaries?

When working though these questions, you might find it helpful to include some feedback from other counsellors who have argued for the inclusion of disclosure:

- I am allowing myself to appear as a fallible human, thereby strengthening our relationship by presenting myself as 'real'.
- I am sharing information to find common ground to improve our bond and build on our relationship.
- Disclosing information demonstrates my congruence and transparency.
- I self-disclose to prove a point.
- Disclosures can demonstrate how I am able to relate to my client's situation.
- It demonstrates my understanding by highlighting our commonalities.
- It offers my client an alternative perspective.

And the points of some who are very much against….

- It is an opportunity for my client to manipulate our sessions.
- My personal information could sway the tone of our sessions and lead to negative developments such as rejection.
- I could over-share, detracting away from my client.

- It can easily blur our boundary issues; focus of session, timing, etc.
- It may increase my vulnerability in an unprofessional way.
- I may regret it.
- I may feel guilty or ashamed afterwards.
- My disclosure may allow my client to judge me.
- My client's session should be about them, not me.
- My client may view my disclosure as a weakness.

These viewpoints can help us decide where we sit with regard to sharing versus over-sharing with our clients. The setting we work within can influence where we set our personal and professional boundaries; for example, the age of our client can determine the level of appropriateness.

WORKING WITH YOUNGER CLIENTS

When working with young people there are different considerations to make bearing in mind their age. As just mentioned, this can be regarding the therapeutic relationship, but also in relation to legal capacity and informed consent. The BACP *Ethical Framework* (2015) states

> 28. Careful consideration will be given to working with children and young people that: a. takes account of their capacity to give informed consent, whether it is appropriate to seek the consent of others who have parental responsibility for the young person, and their best interests b. demonstrates knowledge and skills about ways of working that are appropriate to the young person's maturity and understanding.

Issues relating to Safeguarding can differ depending on whether English or Scots Law is being adhered to. In England and Wales, Gillick competency is accepted case law whereas the guidelines are slightly different under Scots Law. At the time of writing, in Scotland there is a presumption of legal capacity at 12, but that doesn't mean those younger do not have legal capacity. Children can enter counselling without parents' consent as long as they are able to demonstrate that they understand what counselling is and how it might help them. Whichever legal system we adhere to, we still must ensure that all consent is informed. It is therefore important that we give an age-appropriate explanatory leaflet or ask them to sign an age-appropriate contract. Unlike in England, parents cannot revoke their child's decision to attend counselling in Scotland. This is included within the Age of Legal Capacity (Scotland) Act (1991) (S2(4) competence). According to this legislation, the best interest for the child is so subjective that only a court can decide. If you are unsure, read your contract of employment to find out what specific laws you've agreed to adhere to.

There are some definite advantages to working with younger clients, as they may be more comfortable sharing their feelings and thoughts as a result of counselling being more available, accepted and integrated into the mainstream school system. However, from a boundary-testing perspective, they can approach the sessions with a considerably more relaxed fashion. This doesn't necessarily mean that they don't value the sessions or feel committed, just that they might be viewing attendance in a less regimented way.

For counsellors working with this client group, an additional danger might be an over-investment in a younger client. By this I mean it can be hard to resist a sense of parental responsibility which would result in our professional care evolving into a less boundaried relationship. It can be more challenging to remember that our client, whatever their age, comes to us with their own aims, objectives, value base and unique sense of self. It can be difficult to strive to place the client's needs at the centre of the relationship rather than our own, especially if we find it difficult to place ourself in a child's world. How we view the world when young is very different to how we view it later in life, and it can be hard to remember that, especially if we are worried about our young client. The future for that client then becomes about us and not them and this situation should always be acknowledged and addressed in supervision. Finding the right balance between being congruent and being motivated by personal opinion can often benefit from some objective, external input.

UNPLANNED BREAKS

Breaks in the therapeutic contact can create a barrier to our counselling process. There are several valid reasons when we may find our client is forced to accept an unplanned break. Situations might include sessions missed due to either their illness or that of the counsellor, last minute holidays or funding issues. If you rent a therapy room, the landlord might also contribute to missed sessions if the premises are closed for any reason. By discussing unplanned breaks during the original contracting session, and agreeing a strategy for communicating and continuing working together, unplanned breaks can be easily accommodated. However, if the break is due to funding constraints, the resulting plan may well depend upon the setting. In private practice, many counsellors implement a sliding fee scale depending upon the financial status of the client. If the client's financial situation changes during the therapy, it may be that they change to paying a lower rate. However, if the client is being funded by their employer or through a healthcare provider, they may well have to enter a time-consuming re-assessment process before additional funding can be accessed and sessions restored. Individual counsellors may take a risk on the outcome of the re-evaluation and allow a client to continue without a break relying on a positive outcome. Any frustrations that can accompany this employer/employee tension can be explored. However, each situation has different contributing factors and should be discussed openly with our client. To not do so would demonstrate a lack of care and professionalism.

AREAS FOR CONCERN AND POTENTIAL CHALLENGES

When working with challenges, disruption, ruptures and complaints, we are considerably more susceptible to burnout, so our self-care should become a priority. Many counsellors fall into a safe pattern of working where supervision time is spent reflecting on the client relationship and their therapeutic process. The impact of potential challenges can be reduced if we allocate supervision time to plan for the future as well as reflecting on the past and the present. By talking through challenging or disruptive scenarios we haven't yet experienced in our professional practice, we are able to consider our reactions and responses in a non-threatening, non-pressured environment. In addition, an experienced supervisor can also offer the objectivity of their professional insight.

Questions for reflection

1. Have you already experienced boundaries under pressure?
2. If so, what was the effect on your practice?
3. How might you evidence that you have behaved ethically?
4. If a client complains about you, how will you ensure that you respond in a way that adds to, rather than detracts from, your relationship?
5. If you were given a gift by a client, would you feel that it challenged a boundary?

Chapter summary

This chapter has touched on some areas that counsellors can find uncomfortable. Being challenged can see us reacting in ways that we don't expect and it can be difficult to reframe our negative experiences to make sure they inform our practice so it develops and grows. Managing a safe environment whilst maintaining our ability to be flexible and embrace change is possible but must be planned and agreed with our client. Decisions are not to be unilateral but collaborative as a transparent working process reduces the risk of a client feeling disempowered and out of control.

FURTHER READING

Papadopoulos, L., & Cross, M. (2006). What do I do if? Questions commonly asked by trainees. In R. Bor, & M. Watts (eds), *The Trainee Handbook* (2nd edn). London: Sage.

Proctor, G. (2014). *Values and ethics in counselling and psychotherapy.* London: Sage.

9

CLIENT-LED RUPTURES

When we think of challenges in counselling, there are several aspects worth bearing in mind. Firstly, challenges to boundaries can be either intentional or unintentional, conscious or unconscious. Our client might make a comment that they consider irrelevant but we may hear it as being challenging. We can't assume that our client is aware of how their questions or comments may be heard by us. More importantly, as with any behaviour that we interpret or label as challenging, the challenge is to the person on the receiving end – the counsellor and not usually the client. Also, any challenge might simply be a form of communication that indicates an underlying issue. Finally, consideration of the context of the challenge, such as the setting, can have a standing on the situation. For example, a counsellor working in a prison will have different boundary issues and flexibility to a counsellor working within a voluntary organisation or in private practice.

THE DIFFERENT WAYS IN WHICH CLIENTS MIGHT CHALLENGE THE AGREED BOUNDARIES

Our own personal vulnerabilities influence what we interpret as challenging and what we don't. How challenges are presented also has a standing here. If a client is being openly confrontational this can have a very different impact on the therapeutic relationship to a client asking a simple question out of curiosity. It is always helpful to include both the *content* and the *method of asking* when reflecting on challenges.

With regard to how this might be received by the client, Hartmann (1989, 1997; Hartmann, Elking & Mithlesh, 1991; Hartmann, Harrison & Zborowski, 2001) has published some informative papers in which the differing approaches to boundaries are discussed. The concept of 'thickness' and 'thinness' in relation to boundaries was first introduced by Hartmann in 1997 and is a method of measuring how rigid a person's adherence to rules is. A thick score would suggest less flexibility and may focus more on the boundary than on the impact the boundary can have. A thin score may indicate a more malleable approach and a heightened sense of the effect of a boundary. This measuring of respecting boundaries is particularly useful as it highlights not simply how a client might respond to limits within the counselling relationship, but in everyday situations. Awareness and exploration of this can contribute positively to the therapeutic process.

Question for reflection

What potential challenges can you think of? These might include a challenge that you have previously experienced or one that you worry might happen. Consider both obvious, straightforward challenges as well as less obvious, more obtuse ones.

When doing this, it can be helpful to bear in mind the difference between crossing a boundary and a boundary violation (Gabbard, 2005; Zachrisson, 2013).

- Boundary crossings are usually single incidents or risks intended to contribute to the therapy, and open for exploration.
- Boundary violations are damaging or exploitative, serious in nature and not discussed as part of the therapy.

An example of a boundary crossing might be taking the counselling outside the therapy room (Jordan & Marshall, 2010), where the rigid frame of the office or therapy space gives way to a more fluid relationship between the social and the therapeutic world. Whilst intended to break down formal barriers and not endanger the client, taking a walk with a client during their session can add to the therapeutic alliance. This is an approach often adopted if a client isn't able to attend a counselling 'space' but where the counsellor must enter theirs, such as in hospital or addiction services.

THE DILEMMAS RAISED FOR THERAPISTS IN SUCH SITUATIONS

We will inevitably work with clients who hold very different world views and have a different value base to ourselves. All of us have areas that clients raise that make us feel uncomfortable on a personal or professional level. Exploring our discomfort in supervision is the key to examining the situation, our reaction, any possible impact upon the therapeutic relationship, how best to move forward and reflection on how we have developed as a practitioner as a result of this situation.

Essentially, it is an essential device to consider the way we reflect on 'challenge'. We may immediately jump to the conclusion that challenge is questioning, confrontational or difficult. However, if we alter that slightly and view it rather as an invitation to being flexible, client centred and reflexive, the whole situation alters. No longer must we feel like our service, contract, agreement or self is being questioned in a negative way but rather, the client is actively communicating with us to highlight areas that they are finding difficult. The difficulty might be genuinely innocent (*'I'm unable to attend next week as it's my daughter's play at school'*) or alternatively might be a way of demonstrating avoidance of therapeutic development (*'I am annoyed that you won't tell me your opinion of my wife'*). This introduces the aspect of conscious and unconscious challenges. There is often complex communication behind clients' challenges which we can highlight and develop when we have explored their intention further. Is our client aware of their challenge and do they intend to receive it in a particular way? Is it designed to shock, irritate or disempower me? Or is it an unconscious challenge that they are totally unaware of? Whichever it is, rather than avoiding the content and moving on, we can identify it and explore it in our session, thereby using it as a source of learning, whether intentional or not.

Like this, there are some very easy methods to reduce the occurrence of dilemmas and challenges and to reduce the power imbalance. Solutions may be as simple as placing a clock in the room so both counsellor and client can see it equally making the progress of time a shared knowledge rather than a device used to empower the counsellor. Many counselling orientations do not offer advice, but placing information leaflets in the waiting room is an acceptable method to alert the client to practical and external support without compromising any theoretical boundaries.

HOW CLIENT'S PRESENTATIONS AND BEHAVIOUR MIGHT BE UNDERSTOOD AND WORKED WITH IN DIFFERENT THEORETICAL ORIENTATIONS

Counsellors are trained to work within theoretical modalities that provide a framework to underpin their practice. This is to ensure that counsellors are working with recognised and established approaches, techniques and skills that are known to help clients. These different ways of working vary so widely that they have the potential to involve very different boundaries. However, the ethical frameworks introduced by professional bodies are designed to reduce the individual differences between practices and instil a benchmark that their members work within as well. This is in addition to increasing our safe working practices.

Counsellors become very used to working within an environment designed to maintain high professional standards even if they are newly trained because of the boundaries in place during our professional education. Spending one or more years in counselling training means we are aware of course and class boundaries which are in many ways parallel to those we use with clients. As such they can provide insight into how it feels to have rules enforced compared to the flexibility of having an input. When undertaking counselling training it is usual for one of the initial classes to be spent developing a contract which considers how we interact with our fellow students, lecturers, academic and practical work and environment. As this is underpinned by both an ethical framework and professional standards it reduces any doubt or confusion regarding ethos, expectations and relationships. Discussion and agreement with a client at the beginning of a counselling relationship may have many similarities but there can also be significant differences depending upon which theoretical orientation underpins the process.

HUMANISTIC APPROACHES

When trained to work within a humanistic or existential approach, the focus is placed heavily on the client as an autonomous agent and an expert in their own life. There is an acceptance that clients should be empowered to make choices and be free to make their own decisions. May (1992: 20) explains that *'from the psychological point of view, it is essential to believe in freedom in order to have an adequate picture of personality on which to do effective counseling'.* For such freedom to be present in the therapy room the security that agreed boundaries provide is significant. Person-centred counsellors embrace the ideals of organismic valuing, the actualising tendency and self-concept, all of which contribute to the therapeutic process. For example, organismic valuing, whereby one makes decisions based upon their personal experiences, will alter the dynamic between every client and every contracting session. Client A may well have very different priorities to Client B and these can be made obvious when negotiating the limits within which we collaborate. Considering the motivational drive (or actualising tendency) of every client during this first meeting is not easy either – Carl Rogers observed how our clients tend to shift away from external forces and towards self-regulation. People prefer a sense of autonomy and don't like to feel they are being controlled. This is very evident throughout person-centred approach and underpins the methodology used, but it is also a key element to remember when discussing and agreeing a new therapeutic relationship.

Counsellors working within a transactional analysis (TA) model may find contracting takes on an even bigger role. Not only does the process provide an underpinning foundation for the relationship, it is also a core element of the therapeutic technique. There is recognition that the interpersonal interaction between client and counsellor can be influenced by games and transactions. Therefore, the focus on the immediate I–Thou relationship can aid the negotiation process. A core belief within TA, as with other humanistic approaches, is that our clients are perfectly capable of being self-directive and making decisions regarding their own life in relation to their life script. This principle is integrated throughout the relationship, but the use of contracting for change is a key component as a method of establishing commitment. When writing about TA counselling, Stewart (1996: 39) identifies four different kinds of boundaries:

- clear and rigid
- unclear and rigid
- unclear and flexible
- clear and flexible.

This is an excellent framework for considering our transparency and for highlighting how rigid or flexible rules are not always good or bad but can be tools within the counselling process. For example, clear, rigid rules are vital for non-negotiable ground rules. These are fixed and both parties must agree to abide by them if they are to work together. These can include safety issues such as not becoming violent within sessions and security issues such as confidentiality. Alternatively, unclear but rigid parameters can cause confusion, especially if the rigidity is intentional but not shared with the client. This is similar to unclear but flexible rules. They may not be made explicit but are up for negotiation.

Stewart's example of timekeeping in this context highlights how confused a client may become if they are late for a session without being aware of any consequences, or not realising that they are able to alter the time of their session to be more convenient. This can be compared to clear and flexible boundaries which may include the negotiations of a working or business contract which are also common practice in TA and include areas such as how often to meet. If both client and counsellor discuss these operational aspects of the sessions, they should both be more empowered to engage in a shared process that meets the needs of all involved balancing maintaining their safety, adhering to the law, working within policies and procedures as well as professional and ethical guidelines.

COGNITIVE BEHAVIOURAL APPROACHES

Cognitive behavioural approaches, such as Rational Emotional Behavioural Therapy (REBT), Cognitive Therapy (CT) and Cognitive Behavioural Therapy (CBT) adopt a more pragmatic approach with clients, forming a more objective framework. Whitfield and Davidson (2007: 80) acknowledge the key role that clarity in contracting plays when they state '… *the patient has to give informed consent. He or she needs to hear about the structure and time course of the treatment, its benefits and side effects.*' Although a very medically worded statement, this highlights the importance of being honest from the start and not setting up false hope. This sharing of information is not only for the client to understand the boundaries of any session but also to be informed of any expected outcome, ensuring their commitment to engage in the therapy is based on a shared understanding of what is expected to take place.

Any expectation of any additional tasks, homework and extracurricular activities would also be included at this point so the client is aware that the therapy isn't only contained within the sessions, but also practised or tested between sessions. This is summed up by Trower, Jones, Dryden and Casey (2011: 33), who write: '*Success in engaging the client depends to a significant degree on various aspects of preparation before the first meeting.*'

There are similarities here with solution-focused therapies, where time restrictions are often a tool to the process and clients are keenly encouraged to continue working towards their goals between sessions. The collaborative relationship and the respect bestowed on the client when viewed as an expert in their own situation (O'Connell, 2003) can be very powerful and introduce a positive dynamic into the relationship. However, there are quite significant differences to other modalities as the focus of therapy within this approach is very much on the future rather than the past. The client's previous experience is not so key to the process so therapy begins immediately (MacDonald, 2007).

PSYCHODYNAMIC APPROACHES

Establishing and maintaining boundaries within psychodynamic approaches, such as psychoanalysis, analytical therapy and object relations is also very important, although a range of different aspects are also included, such as suitability. Freud talked of psychoanalysis being the most powerful of all psychotherapeutic procedures and therefore, not suitable for all clients (Freud, 2003: 142). This aspect of the suitable and unsuitable client is recognised as an important factor indicating the potential efficacy of therapy (Jacobs, 2004: 69–76), which differs greatly from person-centred counselling, where Roger's response to questions of suitability was '*These questions and others like them, are understandable and legitimate just as it would be reasonable to enquire whether gamma rays would be an appropriate cure for chilblains*'. Rogers felt that attitude, understanding and acceptance were far more accurately indicative of a potentially positive outcome to therapy. With regard to this difference of opinion, Howard emphasises the role of informed consent when explaining psychodynamic processes to make the client aware of the examination of the unconscious so recommends including a discussion on transference and what might be covered during their sessions together (Howard, 2006: 70).

MAINTAINING A SUCCESSFUL COUNSELLING RELATIONSHIP

There is strong evidence to support the most crucial role of the counsellor is to build a stable, trusting and warm relationship with the client. The concept of social connectedness reducing the likelihood of psychological distress is widely documented and the relational element with others is a reoccurring theme when identifying the success within the therapeutic alliance.

From a relational perspective, how might the following five counsellors progress when challenged by these clients?

- Gerry has been working with a shy, quiet client who doesn't feel sufficiently assertive to contribute to their sessions and is monosyllabic when encouraged to talk.
- Amanda feels she is being manipulated by a client who always becomes tearful toward the end of sessions and asks if they can extend the appointment.
- Megan is working with a client who is resistant to boundaries interpreting them as being told what to do.
- Mark confronts you as he believes that you broke confidentiality and disclosed content from your sessions to his doctor.
- During every session, Frances regularly asks her counsellor *'what should I do?'*

By gently identifying the specific challenge and introducing it into the relationship, it is possible to change a challenge into a therapeutic tool. So:

- Gerry might encourage his client with an easy, relaxed pace and ask *'I notice that you're very quiet this week. I'm interested to know your thoughts in more detail.'*
- Amanda could reinforce the time boundary at the beginning of the session and place a clock within view of both. If her client asks to prolong to session, she can explain that it isn't possible but is happy to make another appointment. She could also state her observation *'I notice each week that you begin to become upset near the end of our session together. I wonder what this means for you?'*
- Megan might match her client's directness and focus on what boundaries mean to her client and what aspects she struggles with. This is also an opportunity to re-visit the contract and identify any appropriate flexibility. It is also worth asking if compromise would be helpful or if it would dilute an uncomfortable but altogether more healthy alternative?
- Mark is upset and challenging you openly. This situation demands honesty, openness, fact and revisiting the agreement on confidentiality. It is also an opportunity to encourage Mark to share where exactly his feelings stem from: betrayal, lack of trust, private information, etc.
- Frances is constantly seeking external validation. Here, a focus on Frances' own value base, decision-making process and self-permission would bring her uncertainty into the realm of the therapeutic process.

REDUCING THE THERAPISTS' DILEMMAS

In Chapter 2 we reflected on Davies' description of ethical decision making in the form of a diagram (Davies, 2015: 6). We can now use that definition, along with a model developed by Bond (2010: 227–238), to consider ethical decision making in context, creating a framework to develop our own working, reflective structure. We can use the examples given in Chapter 1 when you were asked to reflect on what you might do in each situation.

- A client consciously or unconsciously ignoring the end of the session and wishing to continue.
- A client's mobile phone ringing.
- A client becoming angry and walking out.
- A client describing events in detail but completely resistant to discussing their feelings.
- A client disclosing abuse.
- A client you suspect is avoiding paying.
- A client admitting that they are attracted to us.
- One client dominating the session in couple's counselling.
- Clients in a group session talking over each other.
- A client wanting to end their sessions as they are finding it too upsetting.

Firstly, if we find we are in a situation that is causing anxiety or concern, it is usually helpful to change our perspective. Consider the situation from a different angle – maybe that of the client, our supervisor, family member or conduct committee. A shift in focus such as this can often help clarify any issue sufficiently to identify positive ways of working. Bond (2010: 227–238) developed a six-step process to work through if in a dilemma managing risk:

1. Produce a brief description of the problem or dilemma.
2. Consider who holds responsibility for resolving the problem.
3. Consider all the relevant ethical and legal guidance.
4. Identify all possible courses of action.
5. Select the best course of action.
6. Evaluate the outcome.

   1) *Producing a brief description of the problem or dilemma* helps you understand exactly what the core of the problem or dilemma is. By condensing it into a short, succinct description it can help you identify the key issue/s and disregard any aspects that aren't directly involved.

2) *Considering who holds responsibility for resolving the problem* is an important step to ascertain exactly whose problem it is. You might make an automatic assumption that it is yours as counsellor, but on closer consideration, it may be the client's problem or raise an issue with out of date policies or procedures. Remember that not all dilemmas are the counsellor's.

3) *When considering all the relevant ethical and legal guidance*, focus on the range of guidance you have available to you bearing in mind that you are a trained professional and a key aspect of your role is to make ethical decisions based on your personal morals, previous experience, as well as your professional ethical framework, current legislation and your organisational policies and procedures. Involving your clinical supervisor is key to this process although it is important to not rely on them to 'solve' the situation but to trust yourself and your judgment once you have examined all the contributing factors.

4) *By identifying all possible courses of action* and viewing the situation more objectively you are more likely to be able to identify options available to you. You may find it helpful to imagine that a colleague is describing the situation to you and asking for your advice. You may prefer to produce a structured list or carry out a random brainstorming session before excluding unfeasible options.

5) *Selecting the best course of action* will be based on a range of contributing factors but a good test is to consider how you would defend it should that be required. If there are any aspects that you are still doubtful of, revisit them. Is your decision appropriate, valid, legal, ethical, helpful, respectful and robust?

6) *Evaluate the outcome* by reflecting back on the process and consider if it was successful, or it might be improved or it highlighted significant areas for further development. If the outcome and the process were successful, remember your approach and strategies in case you are required to use them again. If there were areas for improvement, spend time working through them as soon as possible whilst they are still fresh in your mind. Be clear exactly what might be worked on and who should be involved.

Finally, if you feel that either the outcome or the decision-making process could be significantly improved, be systematic in your dissection of your procedure and methods so that you can approach each element with the clarity required for improving it. Alternatively, you could imagine a colleague describing the situation to you and then asking for your advice. The introduction of objectivity and change in perspective can be very helpful for us to view the problem from an external locus. Hopefully, you have been able to approach the ten dilemmas in a more structured manner.

THERAPEUTIC OPPORTUNITIES PROVIDED BY BOUNDARY CHALLENGES FROM AN UNHAPPY CLIENT

When working in private practice we may find that much of our marketing is via informal word of mouth and recommendation. If a client is unhappy with our work for whatever reason, this can have an impact on our reputation. It is to the benefit of all if we are able to sense when our client is unhappy and broach it with them in a gentle and open manner, avoiding any confrontation, defensiveness or excuses. If our client discloses that they are unhappy, they are unhappy and that's what we need to accept and work with. At no point should we challenge their view, or deny it but rather, accept it as their truth, view it from a professional rather than personal stance and prepare to be adaptable within safe boundaries.

When it comes to being adaptable, Rogers viewed this from the perspective of creativity; he wrote of its contribution to 'the good life' saying that if one is '*likely to adapt and survive under changing environmental conditions he would be able creatively to make sound adjustments to new as well as old conditions*' (Rogers, 1967: 94). If our client is able to explain what they are finding unhelpful, it provides a platform for us to work together to 'make sound adjustments' and rebuild that aspect of our work.

It should be mentioned at this point that a client may complain if they feel they are being taken out of their comfort zone. If you believe that their complaint is arising from developments in the therapeutic process, it can be an indicator that it is time to evaluate and assess their development and change up to this point, so they are able to view their discomfort or unhappiness in a more positive light. If the client is complaining about an element contained within the contract, it may well be an area that can be re-examined and renegotiated; it is a working document designed to protect and meet the needs of client and counsellor. This may be less than straightforward when working within a service with nationally, rather than locally, developed policies and procedures. These may be developed for other aspects of the workplace and not cognisant of practices relating specifically to counselling. If the complaint is personal, it's about you specifically so it can be far more challenging to separate the personal from the professional. Encourage the client to be as clear as possible regarding their issue and it can be helpful to also ask them what they would like to happen next. This provides insight into their present feelings and future hopes for their complaint.

It also helps us understand the issue in some perspective as the client's wish for the next step might be very straightforward and allow us to move through the situation without breaking the therapeutic alliance. Making an appointment with your supervisor prior to any next session would also be advisable for some reflection, guidance or reinforcement. If the situation is such that the client wishes to terminate therapy or requests a referral to follow up their complaint, you still have a responsibility to consider the safety of the client. If you feel the complaint is justified it can be invaluable to work through your options and choices with your supervisor. If you feel the complaint isn't justified, the ability to provide evidence of your decision-making process becomes crucial. Having a clear justification for your working practices isn't about avoiding litigation or 'watching your back' but rather, being a robust and professional practitioner who is able to evidence the motivations underlying what you do and how you do it, in the therapy room.

CHALLENGES THIS CAN RAISE FOR CLIENTS

Open communication is the bedrock of a successful working relationship, so a client who isn't happy or comfortable is going to respond in one of three ways.

1. This might be in a healthy way, letting us know so that we can discuss it openly, examining the reasons and contributing factors and then searching together for alternative ways of working that might be more successful.
2. It might also be in a way that is less collaborative such as just not coming back, cancelling future appointments or making a complaint.
3. Alternatively, an unhappy client who feels disempowered may internalise the issue, remain silent but disengage with the process. If the relationship has been open and supportive to this point, it may be that the client raises the issue with us directly but if the relationship has broken down, they may raise the complaint elsewhere.

WORKING WITH COMPLAINTS

During the contracting session, clients should be made aware of, and given a copy of, the complaints procedure. This is essential if we wish to avoid disempowering them should they be unhappy. If we are working within a wider service they may wish to contact our line manager and if not, they may escalate their complaint by formally contacting our professional body. Both routes can be challenging for all involved. The client may worry about not being taken seriously, not being heard, or colleagues colluding to protect the counsellor.

We have already talked about challenges that the client might instigate, but what are the challenges to the counsellor in dealing with these? There is often a fear that flexibility can be interpreted as weakness or 'giving in', such as when a toddler has a tantrum in the aisle of a supermarket. However, this might be an automatic response that is not based on any evidence. If we start from the stance that our client isn't intentionally being obtuse or trying to upset us, then being transparent and open to change isn't difficult. However, of course, there are still areas that are not open to flexibility such as those dictated by law, our ethical guidelines, our theoretical orientation or our policies and procedures. The more open and clear our initial contracting session, the fewer issues should arise with these. There are many areas that are less clear. Consider the situations below:

- Susie feels lost and asks you to advise her what to do.
- Jeremy wants to bring his partner to the next session so you can meet him.
- Rose has missed two sessions without contacting you.
- You bump into Philippa in the street and she starts introducing you to her family.

Questions for reflection

1. What clues might your clients give to show they are experiencing dissatisfaction?
2. How might you approach assessing and re-negotiating boundaries with an unhappy client?
3. When did you last visit your current policies and procedures?

Chapter summary

How we interpret a challenge may differ greatly from the client's intention. It is helpful to view the situation as challenging as inviting change rather than being an intentional challenge. Our clients may be questioning, disagreeing or requesting something different consciously or unconsciously and getting to the bottom of their communication can provide us and them with insight into wider issues. Overall, challenge is good for developing the efficacy of therapy.

FURTHER READING

Brown, R., & Stobart, K. (2008). *Understanding boundaries and containment in clinical practice*. London: Karnac.

Hartmann, E. (1997). The concept of boundaries in counselling and psychotherapy. *British Journal of Guidance and Counselling, 25*(3), 147–162.

Wesley, R., Hankin, S., & Stern, J. (2001). *Succeeding with difficult clients: applications of cognitive appraisal therapy*. London: Academic Press.

10

BOUNDARIES AND GOOD PRACTICE IN ACTION

Boundaries don't just define the safe environment in which therapeutic work can take place, as working actively with the boundaries themselves can be a powerful agent of therapeutic change. How our client perceives a safe environment might seem obvious but it isn't always; one client may look for security in guidance, advice and a more medical approach from a professional they view as an expert while another client might resent that greatly and expect a more client-centred approach, where they themselves are seen as the centre of expertise in their own life. It takes confidence and skill to develop the ability to create an environment and positive relationship that integrates the limits of our work. It is essential that we resist leaving our contract in the past and use it as an ongoing presence in the relationship.

BOUNDARIES PROVIDE A SAFE ENVIRONMENT

There are many therapeutic reasons for working with, as opposed to being limited by, boundaries. Along with our theoretical orientation, use of skills and therapeutic alliance, boundaries contribute to our management and practice of therapy. One of the underpinning motivators for this may well involve issues of control. It is well recognised that one of the major contributors to stress is a perceived or actual lack of control (Sainfort, 1991), which applies within all aspects of life, including within counselling. Involving our client throughout the process encourages empowerment and affords the client a sense of maintaining control of the organisation of the sessions. Avoiding taking complete control, and allowing the client to contribute, may have two significant advantages: first, it shows the client that you are keen to increase equality and empowerment; and second, collaborative working can contribute to the therapeutic process itself. This happens because the client is able to identify the difference a level of autonomy has on their wellbeing, which can then be replicated outside the therapy room. We want to give an equal amount of control to the client, giving them a sense of ownership, resulting in the increased likelihood of them investing and committing to the process. A perceived lack of control leads to stress, resentment and a distancing from the process, which would not only be unhealthy and unhelpful, but also unethical; we wouldn't be putting our client and their needs first.

Of course, there is the risk of an imbalance: in some settings, a client may feel they have too little power and no opportunity to contribute, no sense of autonomy and too little understanding resulting in a lower sense of self-worth or value. Essentially, feeling like a cork bobbing out of control in the therapy ocean. At the other end of the scale, too much input from a client who doesn't fully understand the consequences of particular boundaries will be unsafe and unprofessional. It may result in limits that aren't helpful, illegal or unethical and suggest a definite, unhealthy imbalance in the relationship. To gain a successful, healthy balance that reinforces the therapeutic alliance, we need to work actively with our boundaries to integrate the three interdependent aspects of goals, tasks and bonds (Bordin, 1979). With the goals being determined by the client and the tasks being agreed by both counsellor and client as being helpful for achieving the goals, the bond is the development of confidence and trust that results from successful progress.

WORKING ACTIVELY WITH BOUNDARIES

We have already established that our boundaries are intended to maintain safety, but that they can be developed and tweaked with agreement throughout the counselling process. It is undeniable that the therapist has a substantial amount of power and responsibility when doing this, but this can be a positive aspect that makes the most of working with boundaries in the service of the client. Encouraging our client to reflect upon and evaluate our initial agreement becomes part of the therapy itself. Being in a situation where a decision must be made involves a range of cognitive processes that, with support, can build on and reinforce the working alliance. These cognitive processes can be framed as being transferable, thereby not just confined to the counselling relationship, but applicable in everyday life too. An example of this would be a discussion on roles. In the counselling room, being clear about roles, rights and responsibilities can be fairly structured and clear cut but there can be a parallel process for the client. They may find that having a similar discussion in a problematic relationship at home might be a way of using an experience in a very practical way. We can use Philip as an example of how the process of contracting with a counsellor can inform our contracting in other ways.

Philip made an appointment with a counsellor in private practice. He was experiencing difficulties with his family relationships, is at the end of his tether and is considering moving out. He has been married to Sharon for 22 years and they have two children, Ruby who is 17 and Matt who is 15. Both Ruby and Matt have been challenging the boundaries that were agreed at home and the school have been in touch as their school work is suffering. Last week Ruby was brought home by the police when they found her and her friends drinking alcohol in a bus stop in the centre of town and Matt has been missing school to play computer games at his friend's house. When Philip and Sharon attempted to discuss this situation and agree on a consequence, they couldn't agree on an approach. Philip was furious and wanted to punish both of them to teach them a lesson but Sharon reminded him that he had behaved in a similar way at that age and she believed it was just part of growing up. Philip explained that this happens all the time and he doesn't trust Sharon as she colludes with the children. She doesn't support anything that he says in front of them and he is sure that she doesn't when he's not there. He feels frustrated, angry, isolated and disconnected.

The contracting process was fairly straightforward and Philip and his counsellor were both comfortable with their agreement. It was during the next session that Philip began to realise that the roles within his family were unclear. He saw himself as the head of the family and ultimately responsible, which differed significantly from Sharon who saw the family as a team. Philip decided that an honest discussion with Sharon about how he felt might be a first step to them agreeing on an approach to parenting.

Philip attended 19 sessions and eventually he and Sharon were able to find a middle ground that involved a team approach with agreed punishments, that both felt were appropriate for the situation.

The counsellor found that the counselling contract became the core focus for almost every session, as Philip realised that the structure and clarity that evolved from an overt agreement gave him a sense of control and a plan to follow which benefitted his familial relationships.

WORKING POSITIVELY WITH BOUNDARIES AND ATTACHMENT

Our practice modality will significantly influence our placing of boundaries within our counselling relationship. For example, a therapist adhering to a medical model may be considerably more directive than a counsellor working to a client-centred model. Therefore, our agreement, negotiation and use of boundaries may vary considerably to that of a colleague's. Bordin's (1979) work, exploring the strength of the therapeutic alliance, informs us of the need to actively examine and understand the client's attitudes to rules based on their experience and upbringing. Whatever our orientation, this may highlight their conscious and unconscious urges which, by bringing them into the client's awareness, may pinpoint any relevance to the current situation. When working with a client who has experienced attachment issues we require a greater awareness and sensitivity to any transference between a past experience and the present relationship. Although Freud stated that '*the transference, which, whether affectionate or hostile, seemed in every case to constitute the greatest threat to the treatment, becomes its best tool, by whose help the most secret compartments of mental life can be opened*' (Freud, 1917: 444), it is not just in psychodynamic modalities that a re-playing of past responses can occur. If the bond between our client and ourselves comes under the spotlight, it can be an opportunity to explore previous secure and insecure attachments. This offers our client the time to compare similarities and differences between their past, present and future, empowering them to use new realisations to inform relationships.

COGNITIVE DISTORTIONS IN BOUNDARY MANAGEMENT

Unfortunately, our approach and perception of boundary management is not always rational, logical and in perspective. Being as human as our clients, there will be times within our sessions, both with new clients and with known, when we experience illogical and unhelpful thoughts.

Table 10.1

Cognitive distortion	How it may be experienced by counsellor	A healthier response
Discounting the positives (dismissing constructive aspects)	'My client told me he is starting to make sense of his situation. That won't last.'	'I'm so pleased that my client's situation is clearer. Next week I'll find out how he got on.'
Control fallacies (what others do and feel is my fault)	'Why isn't my client feeling relaxed this week? I must be doing something wrong.'	'I hope my client's strategy to feel less pressured is successful.'
Jumping to conclusions (such as mind reading or fortune telling)	'My client told me she sometimes writes about our sessions on Facebook. She must be criticising me.'	'My client feels secure in letting others know that she's attending counselling.'
Catastrophising (the situation is a crisis)	'My client told me that they'd contacted BACP to ask a question. They will have been making a complaint about me.'	'What an engaged client to show such initiative and clarify details with a professional body. I'll check that he's happy with our work at our next session.'
Blaming (others are responsible for our feelings)	'My client is making me feel unprofessional.'	'Why has this session left me feeling unprofessional? I'll take it to supervision.'
Polarised thinking (extremes with no middle ground)	'My client has been made redundant. She won't be able to afford sessions unless I offer them for free.'	'My client is in a difficult position. We will discuss how she sees counselling fitting in to her future.'
Emotional reasoning (all feelings reflect real life)	'I am feeling a strong attraction to my client. I think this is love'	'I'm feeling a strong attraction to my client. I'll discuss why I am experiencing this with my supervisor, and how it can be used appropriately in the therapy.'
Labelling (apportioning assumed behaviours and attitudes based on a classification e.g. diagnosis)	'There's little chance my client will carry out his plan this week as he's quite low so won't be motivated.'	'My client attended on time this week despite feeling low. He demonstrated his ability to challenge his low mood.'
Mental filtering (focusing on a negative detail to the exclusion of positive ones)	'My client mentioned that this week wasn't as helpful as previous weeks. What did I do wrong?'	'My client has been steadily improving. It's only to be expected that progress will vary session to session.'
Magnification or minimisation (distorting the proportion of the situation)	'My client asked me out this week. I'll think about it as it's only for a coffee.'	'My client wants to spend more time with me so an aspect of our relationship is working but I'll have to remind them of our relational boundaries at the beginning of the next session.'

For some, this can be an exhausting and soul destroying experience, which is why self-care and supervision are so important in helping us to remain professionally and personally boundaried. Some examples of faulty processing of situations with clients that could result in overly critical judgments is shown in Table 10.1.

USING SUPERVISION TO SUPPORT ETHICAL PRACTICE

Our clients expect us, as counsellors, to be able to work with emotional and psychological challenges, overcome perceived and real barriers and connect with their internal and external worlds. So, if we are trained in skills to harness these situations with them, we can be equally as capable of doing the same with ourselves. Exploring options, reflecting on practice, re-framing and sharing decision-making processes is not a sign of weakness or inability to cope, but a sign of professional responsibility and personal strength.

If, and when, we experience a lack of confidence or self-doubt that goes beyond healthy reflection, there are several ways to regain perspective. It can sometimes feel overwhelming or impossible to successfully reframe unhelpful subjectivity back into helpful objectivity but the key comes from identifying and understanding any personal or professional meaning the situation has for ourselves. We have a duty to ourselves to identify our own needs. To do that, we often require guidance from a number of external sources which might include:

- Supervisor.
- Colleagues.
- Professional support network.
- Professional body.
- Current literature.

When interviewing and choosing an appropriate supervisor, we might find ourselves torn between practical requirements, such as how close is their office, how much do they charge and do they have experience in the sector in which I work? We may then move onto a secondary list which includes: Do I like them? Do I trust them? What model of supervision do they practise? It isn't until we begin working with them that we start to discover how they structure sessions, challenge us, encourage and support us. This may all mirror our own client's experience with us, but we have the added opportunity to search out a supervisor who will work with our needs. This doesn't mean a supervisor who lets us remain in our comfort zone, nor one who is harsh and overly critical, but one that understands our strengths and weaknesses and stretches us into what Vygotsky referred to as our 'zone of proximal development' (Vygotsky, 1978: 32) He may well have been writing about the development of children, but there are certainly times when this theory feels very fitting for a counsellor attending supervision! To be supported while identifying what can be done alone, what can be done with guidance and what cannot be done can be very helpful.

Working with a supervisor who recognises and values our strengths, abilities and skills goes some way to ensure that they see us as an equal: a fellow practitioner with a slightly different role. What we know is not helpful, is a supervisor who views themselves as the expert or master to our role as apprentice. We might also find that choosing a supervisor who works with the same theoretical orientation to us, doesn't automatically guarantee the best fit. When it comes to working successfully with boundaries, it can be highly insightful to hear different methods, approaches and justifications which can be offered by a practitioner working with an alternative modality.

The aim and structure of our supervision can also shape the way we support our clients. By choosing a supervisor by some characteristic other than theoretical orientation, such as a model based on development, education or monitoring, we can adopt a balance between supporting and challenging what we do. This is demonstrating our ability to take responsibility, to establish and maintain management of our own boundaries in a manner that reinforces our own self-care.

THE IMPORTANCE OF SELF-AWARENESS AND SELF-CARE IN DEVELOPING CAPACITY TO WORK WITH BOUNDARIES

In addition to supervision, we might mirror approaches we adopt with our clients, such as viewing ourself holistically to gain a greater perspective of the current situation. Acquiring the objectivity necessary to respond appropriately to dilemma or challenge, can take time and experience to develop. Developing a tool or structure to use when under pressure can help provide the distance required to disentangle the personal from the professional.

In addition to professional approaches, there are other, general non-work-related methods we can harness to reduce our stress and increase distance which might help us meet our own internal needs:

- Meditation.
- Mindfulness.
- Relaxation.
- Keeping a journal.
- Reading.
- Socialising.
- Exercise.

These interventions can allow us space to acknowledge the difference between whose challenge it is; that often the boundaries under pressure are not our own boundaries, but professional requirements that compromise the wants, not the needs, of our client. To be comfortable knowing when to say 'no' when needed, in a kind yet firm manner can be freeing.

PROACTIVE RATHER THAN REACTIVE BOUNDARY MANAGEMENT OF SELF

Boundary maintenance isn't only in the arena of client work, but in the wider context of practising counselling. Avoiding overwork can be extremely challenging, especially if self-employed when the financial pressures can be immense. Additional pressures include: covering for an absent colleague; attend care team meetings; complete paperwork; and update records, all of which can extend the therapeutic hour to a considerably longer time. Adhering to a personal maximum number of daily or weekly sessions, maintaining clear, current, detailed records, engaging in regular CPD and liaising with colleagues can all help lighten the load and reduce a sense of feeling overwhelmed.

RESEARCH AROUND BOUNDARIES

When it comes to making decisions, there has been much research around the general area of developing and maintaining boundaries: establishing appropriate boundaries, boundary crossing, boundary violations and complaints. This affords us the opportunity to ensure that our own practice is safe, robust and evidence based. Here are four studies, all conducted around different aspects of boundaries:

Counselling environment

If considering the environment that therapeutic contact takes place in, and the potential for 'walk and talk' therapy, Jordan and Marshall (2010: 345–359) focused on evaluating the possibility of delivering counselling and psychotherapy in a more natural setting outside a therapy room. Contracting, potential dilemmas and differences to more traditional settings are central to their paper which introduces an opportunity to re-evaluate our (possibly) automatic routine of working from an office environment.

Boundary violations

In relation to boundary violations, Symons, Khele, Rogers, Turner and Wheeler (2011: 257–265) explored allegations of serious profes-sional misconduct by analysing complaints to the BACP between 1998 and 2007. Using BACP data, they identified 91 cases, within which a significant over-representation of male counsellors was noted. They found that the largest number of cases (25%) were in relation to 'bringing the reputation of counselling/psychotherapy into disrepute'. The study also discovered that lay people were under-represented in the reporting of serious misconduct.

Sexual attraction

Also in 2011, Martin, Godfrey, Meekums and Madill (2011: 248–256) investigated managing boundaries under pressure in relation to sexual attraction, with the aim of identifying therapists' views of sexual boundaries and the strategies employed to manage them. Despite only interviewing 13 experienced therapists, they identified general stages of reacting to boundary pressure:

- 'noting' whereby the counsellor became aware of an attraction
- 'facing up to it personally', by placing ones' self in the situation
- 'reflecting', where exploration of their involvement takes place
- 'processing', where personal and professional implications are considered
- 'formulating and working for client benefit', where the situation is framed in terms of the client's therapeutic process.

The research also identified four types of reaction to boundary pressure in relation to sexual attraction. These were:

1. Self-protective/defensive.
2. Moralising/omnipotent.
3. Neediness/over-identification.
4. Over-protective anxiety.

All four reactions highlighted the dilemmas and tensions counsellors can face when in this situation. An appropriate path has to be found between closeness and distance which even experienced therapists can find particularly challenging.

Clinical decision making

Once aware of a potential boundary challenge, the ensuing clinical decision making and the role of intuition within the process, is the focus of research by Fox, Hagedorn and Sivo (2016). Using video clips of counselling sessions, the decision making of 44 experienced practitioners was explored, resulting in the conclusion that experienced practitioners rely on their experiential knowledge or 'clinical intuition'.

These papers offer the following conclusions. What are your initial thoughts about each and why?

- Counselling in a natural surrounding requires different boundaries.
- Therapy outside is no better or worse than therapy indoors.
- Men are over represented in BACP recorded complaints.
- Most complaints are raised by people already involved in counselling.
- It is problematic and risky for gay counsellors to disclose their sexual orientation to a heterosexual client.
- A participant–observer stance is essential for managing threats to boundaries.
- Boundary crossing is perceived as leading to boundary violation.

These examples may reinforce a fact that we already know, but equally, by reading findings and conclusions, we can be challenged to step out of our comfort zone and try something with our client that is new and creative, but evaluated and safe.

Questions for reflection

1. How comfortable are you with change and therapeutic risk?
2. What are your current strategies for self-care?

(Continued)

(Continued)

3. Which strategies work and which could be more helpful?
4. What are your thoughts surrounding non-office-based therapy?
5. To what extent do you rely on your experiential knowledge and 'clinical intuition' when working with boundary management?

Chapter summary

This chapter has introduced the possibility that boundaries may well be about safety but can also be developmental and worked with in a positive manner to support our client. Even the therapeutic environment in which we work can be flexible if we view it as such. Integrating our contract into our counselling can keep us working actively and positively and avoiding the danger of a predictable, stale practice. As long as we are rigorous in our approach to self-care and supervision, we can be proactive rather than reactive to our client work, as long as it is evidence based and safe.

FURTHER READING

BACP (2015). *Ethical framework for good practice in counselling and psychotherapy*. Lutterworth: BACP.

Fox, J., Hagedorn, W.B., & Sivo, S.A. (2016). Clinical decision-making and intuition: a task analysis of 44 experienced counsellors. *Counselling and Psychotherapy Research*, 16(4): 233–318.

Jordan, M., & Marshall, H. (2010). Taking counselling and psychotherapy outside: destruction or enrichment of the therapeutic frame? *European Journal of Psychotherapy & Counselling*, 12(4): 345–359.

Martin, C., Godfrey, M., Meekums, B., & Madill, A. (2011). Managing boundaries under pressure: a qualitative study of therapists' experiences of sexual attraction in therapy. *Counselling and Psychotherapy Research*, 11(4): 248–256.

Palmer Barnes, F., & Murdin, L. (eds) (2001). *Values and ethics in the practice of psychotherapy and counselling*. Buckingham: Open University Press.

Symons, C., Khele, S., Rogers, J., Turner, J., & Wheeler, S. (2011). Allegations of serious professional misconduct: an analysis of the British Association for Counselling and Psychotherapy's Article 4.6 cases, 1998–2007. *Counselling and Psychotherapy Research*, 11(4): 257–265.

REFERENCES

CHAPTER 1

BACP (n.d.). *What is counselling and psychotherapy?* [online]. Lutterworth: BACP. Available at: www.bacp.co.uk/crs/Training/ whatiscounselling.php (accessed 10 April 2016).

BACP (2015). *Ethical framework for the counselling professions* [online]. Lutterworth: BACP. Available at: www.bacp.co.uk/admin/ structure/files/pdf/14237_ethical-framework-jun15-final.pdf (accessed 13 April 2016).

Kent, R. (2012). *What do counsellors and psychotherapists mean by 'professional boundaries'?* Lutterworth: BACP.

Rogers, C.R. (1964). Toward a modern approach to values: the valuing process in the mature person. *Journal of Abnormal and Social Psychology*, 68(2), 160–167.

CHAPTER 2

BABCP (2010). *Standards of conduct, performance and ethics* [online]. Bury: BABCP. Available at: www.babcp.com/files/About/BABCP-Standards-of-Conduct-Performance-and-Ethics.pdf (accessed 13 April 2016).

Berne, E. (1961). *Transactional analysis in psychotherapy: a systematic individual and social psychiatry.* New York: Grove Press.

Bond, T. (2010) *Standards and ethics for counselling in action* (3rd edn). London: Sage.

Bond, T., & Mitchels, B. (2008). *Confidentiality and record keeping in counselling and psychotherapy.* London: Sage.

BPS (2009). *Code of ethics and conduct* [online]. Available at: www.bps. org.uk/system/files/Public%20files/aa%20Standard%20Docs/inf94_ code_web_ethics_conduct.pdf (accessed 13 April 2016).

Davies, N. (2015). *Ethical decision making within the counselling professions.* Lutterworth: BACP.

HPC (2008). *Standards of conduct, performance and ethics.* London: HPC.

Luft, J., & Ingham, H. (1955). The Johari window, a graphic model of interpersonal awareness. *Proceedings of the Western Training Laboratory in Group Development.* Los Angeles, CA: University of California.

Reamer, F.G. (2013). *Boundary issues and dual relationships in the human services.* New York: Columbia University Press.

Rogers, C.R. (1975). Empathic: an unappreciated way of being. *The Counseling Psychologist, 5,* 2–10.

UKCP (2009). *Ethical principles and code of professional conduct.* Available at: www.psychotherapy.org.uk/UKCP_Documents/stand ards_and_guidance/32_UKCP_Ethical_Principles_and_Code_of_ Professional_Conduct_approved_by_BOT_Sept_09.pdf

CHAPTER 3

BACP (2015). *Ethical framework for the counselling professions* [online]. Lutterworth: BACP. Available at: www.bacp.co.uk/admin/structure/ files/pdf/14237_ethical-framework-jun15-final.pdf (accessed 13 April 2016).

Dale, H. (2016). *Good practice in Action 039: commonly asked questions resource: making the contract within the counselling professions.* Lutterworth: BACP.

Davies, N. (2015). *Ethical decision making within the counselling professions.* Lutterworth: BACP.

ODE (2010). *Oxford dictionary of English* (3rd edn). Oxford: Oxford University Press.

Scottish Government (2014). *The national guidance for child protection in Scotland.* Edinburgh: Scottish Government.

CHAPTER 4

Adults with Incapacity (Scotland) Act (2000). Available at: http://www. legislation.gov.uk/asp/2000/4/contents (accessed 14 February 2017).

Bond, T., & Mitchels, B. (2008). *Confidentiality and record keeping in counselling and psychotherapy.* London: Sage.

GMC (2016). *Sharing information within the healthcare team or with others providing care.* Available at: www.gmc-uk.org/guidance/ ethical_guidance/confidentiality_24_35_disclosing_information_ with_consent.asp (accessed 22 March 2016).

Gov.UK (2005). *Mental Capacity Act.* Available at: www.legislation.gov. uk/ukpga/2005/9/contents (accessed 3 September 2016).

Gov.UK (2015). *Data protection*. Available at: www.gov.uk/data-protection/the-data-protection-act (accessed 7 February 2016).

Mental Capacity Act (Northern Ireland) (2016). Available at: www.legislation.gov.uk/nia/2016/18/contents/enacted (accessed 14 February 2017).

Prevention of Terrorism Act (2005). Available at: www.legislation.gov.uk/ukpga/2005/2/contents (accessed 14 February 2014).

Rogers, C.R. (1961). *On becoming a person*. Boston, MA: Houghton Mifflin.

The Suicide Act (1961). Available at: www.legislation.gov.uk/ukpga/Eliz2/9-10/60/contents (accessed 14 February 2017).

UKCP (2009). *Ethical principles and code of professional conduct*. London: UKCP.

CHAPTER 5

American Psychological Association (2002). *Ethical principles for psychologists and code of conduct*. American Psychological Association. Available at: www.apa.org/ethics (accessed 19 April 2016).

Amis, K. (2011). *Becoming a counsellor: a student companion*. London: Sage.

BACP (2015). *Ethical framework for the counselling professions* [online]. Lutterworth: BACP. Available at: www.bacp.co.uk/admin/structure/files/pdf/14237_ethical-framework-jun15-final.pdf (accessed 13 April 2016).

Bond, T. (2010). *Standards and ethics for counselling in action* (3rd edn). London: Sage.

BPS (2009). *Statement of ethics and conduct*. Leicester: BPS.

UKCP (2009). *Ethical principles and code of professional conduct*. London: UKCP.

CHAPTER 6

BABCP (2010). *Standards of conduct, performance and ethics*. Bury: BABCP.

BACP (2015). *Ethical framework for the counselling professions* [online]. Lutterworth: BACP. Available at: www.bacp.co.uk/admin/structure/files/pdf/14237_ethical-framework-jun15-final.pdf (accessed 13 April 2016).

BPS (2009). *Code of ethics and conduct*. Leicester: BPS.

Breuer, J., & Freud, S. (1895). *Studies in Hysteria* (N. Luckhurst, trans.) (2004). New York: Penguin.

COSCA (2014). *Statement of ethics and code of practice*. Stirling: COSCA.

Egan, G. (2013). *The skilled helper: a problem-management and opportunity-development approach to helping.* San Francisco, CA: Cengage Learning.

Freud, S. (1912). Recommendations to physicians practising psychoanalysis. In *Standard Edition of the Complete Psychological Works of Sigmund Freud* (vol. 12) (J. Strachey, trans.) (1958) (pp. 109–120). London: Hogarth Press.

Giovazolias, T., & Davis, P. (2001). How common is sexual attraction towards clients? The experiences of sexual attraction of counselling psychologists towards their clients and its impact on the therapeutic process. *Counselling Psychology Quarterly, 14*(4), 281–286.

Hermann, M.A., & Robinson-Kurpius, S. (2006). New guidelines on dual relationships. *Counseling Today.* Available at: www.ct.counseling. org/2006/12/new-guidelines-on-dual-relationships/.

Moore, J., & Jenkins, P. (2012). 'Coming out' in therapy? Perceived risks and benefits of self-disclosure of sexual orientation by gay and lesbian therapists to straight clients. *Counselling and Psychotherapy Research, 12*(4), 308–315.

Stewart, W. (2005). *An A–Z of counselling theory and practice.* Cheltenham: Nelson Thornes.

UKCP (2009). *Ethical principles and code of professional conduct.* London: UKCP.

Wosket, V. (1999). *The therapeutic use of self.* London: Routledge.

Yakeley, J. (2014). Psychodynamic therapy: contemporary Freudian approach. In W. Dryden, & A. Reeves (eds), *The handbook of individual therapy* (6th edn). London: Sage.

CHAPTER 7

Amis, K. (2008) Working with client dependency. In W. Dryden, & A. Reeves (eds), *Key issues for counselling in action.* London: Sage.

BACP (2015). *Ethical framework for the counselling professions* [online]. Lutterworth: BACP. Available at: www.bacp.co.uk/admin/ structure/files/pdf/14237_ethical-framework-jun15-final.pdf (accessed 13 April 2016).

BPS (2009). *Code of ethics and conduct.* Leicester: BPS.

CHAPTER 8

BACP (2015). *Ethical framework for the counselling professions* [online]. Lutterworth: BACP. Available at: www.bacp.co.uk/admin/structure/

files/pdf/14237_ethical-framework-jun15-final.pdf (accessed 13 April 2016).

Bond, T. (2010). *Standards and ethics for counselling in action* (3rd edn). London: Sage.

CHAPTER 9

Bond, T. (2010). *Standards and ethics for counselling in action* (3rd edn). London: Sage.

Davies, N. (2015). *Ethical decision making within the counselling professions.* Lutterworth: BACP.

Freud, S. (1933). *An outline of psychoanalysis.* London: Penguin Classics. (Translation of *Neue folge der vorlesungen zur einfuhrung in die psychoanalyse,* 2003.)

Gabbard, G.O. (2005). Patient–therapist boundary issues. *Psychiatric Times, 22*(12).

Hartmann, E. (1989). Boundaries of dreams, boundaries of dreamers: thin and thick boundaries as a new personality measure. *Psychiatric Journal of the University of Ottawa, 14*(4), 557–560.

Hartmann, E. (1997). The concept of boundaries in counselling and psychotherapy. *British Journal of Guidance & Counselling, 25*(2), 147–162.

Hartmann, E., Elkin, R., & Mithlesh, G. (1991). Personality and dreaming: the dreams of people with very thick or very thin boundaries. *Dreaming, 1*(4), 311–324.

Hartmann, E., Harrison, R., & Zborowski, M. (2001). Boundaries in the mind: past research and future directions. *North American Journal of Psychology, 3*: 347–368.

Howard, S. (2006). *Psychodynamic counselling in a nutshell.* London: Sage.

Jacobs, M. (2004). *Psychodynamic counselling in action.* London: Sage.

Jordan, M., & Marshall, H. (2010). Taking counselling and psychotherapy outside: destruction or enrichment of the therapeutic frame? *European Journal of Psychotherapy and Counselling, 12*(4), 345–359.

MacDonald, A. (2007). *Solution-focused therapy: theory, research and practice.* London: Sage.

May, R. (1992). *The art of counselling.* London: Souvenir Press (E & A Ltd).

O'Connell, B. (2003). Introduction to the solution-focused approach. In B. O'Connell, & S. Palmer (eds), *Handbook of solution-focused therapy.* London: Sage.

Rogers, C. (1967). *On becoming a person: a therapist's view of psychotherapy.* London: Constable.

Stewart, I. (1996). *Developing transactional analysis counselling*. London: Sage.

Trower, P., Jones, J., Dryden, W., & Casey, A. (2011). *Cognitive behavioural counselling in action*. London: Sage.

Whitfield, G., & and Davidson, A. (2007). *Cognitive behavioural therapy explained*. Oxon: Radcliffe.

Zachrisson, A. (2013). Ethical breaches and deviations of method in psychoanalysis: a heuristic model for the differentiation of boundary transgressions in psychoanalytic work. *International Forum for Psychoanalysis*, *23*(4), 246–252.

CHAPTER 10

Bordin, E. (1979). The generalizability of the psychoanalytic concept of the working alliance. *Psychotherapy: Theory, Research and Practice*, *16*, 252–260.

Fox, J., Hagedorn, W.B., & Sivo, S.A. (2016). Clinical decision-making and intuition: a task analysis of 44 experienced counsellors. *Counselling and Psychotherapy Research*. doi:10.1002/capr.12084.

Freud, S. (1917). *Transference*. Introductory Lectures on Psychoanalysis (Part III). London: Vintage/The Hogarth Press.

Jordan, M., & Marshall, H. (2010). Taking counselling and psychotherapy outside: destruction or enrichment of the therapeutic frame? *European Journal of Psychotherapy & Counselling*, *12*(4), 345–359.

Martin, C., Godfrey, M., Meekums, B., & Madill, A. (2011). Managing boundaries under pressure: a qualitative study of therapists' experiences of sexual attraction in therapy. *Counselling and Psychotherapy Research*, *11*(4), 248–256.

Sainfort, P.C. (1991). Stress, job control and other job elements: a study of office workers. *International Journal of Industrial Ergonomics*, *7*(1), 11–23.

Symons, C., Khele, S., Rogers, J., Turner, J., & Wheeler, S. (2011). Allegations of serious professional misconduct: an analysis of the British Association for Counselling and Psychotherapy's Article 4.6 cases, 1998–2007. *Counselling and Psychotherapy Research*, *11*(4), 257–265.

Vygotsky, L. (1978). Interaction between learning and development. In M. Gauvain, & M. Cole (eds), *Readings on the development of children* (2nd edn). New York: W.H. Freeman & Co.

INDEX